The Unintended Consequences of High-Stakes Testing

The Unintended Consequences of High-Stakes Testing

M. Gail Jones, Brett D. Jones,
and Tracy Y. Hargrove

ROWMAN & LITTLEFIELD PUBLISHERS, INC.
Lanham • Boulder • New York • Oxford

0742526267

ROWMAN & LITTLEFIELD PUBLISHERS, INC.

Published in the United States of America
by Rowman & Littlefield Publishers, Inc.
A Member of the Rowman & Littlefield Publishing Group
4501 Forbes Blvd., Suite 200, Lanham, Maryland 20706
www.rowmanlittlefield.com

P.O. Box 317, Oxford OX2 9RU, United Kingdom

British Library Cataloguing in Publication Information Available

Library of Congress Cataloging-in-Publication Data
Jones, M. Gail, 1955–
   The unintended consequences of high-stakes testing / M. Gail Jones,
Brett D. Jones, and Tracy Y. Hargrove.
      p.   cm.
   Includes bibliographical references (p.   ) and index.
   ISBN 0-7425-2626-7 (cloth : alk. paper) — ISBN 0-7426-2627-5 (pbk. :
alk paper)
   1. Educational tests and measurements—United States—Evaluation.   2.
Educational tests and measurements—Social aspects—United States.   I.
Jones, Brett D., 1969–   II. Hargrove, Tracy, 1965–   III. Title
LB3051 .J584 2003
371.26'4   2002153819

Printed in the United States of America

♾ ™ The paper used in this publication meets the minimum requirements of
American National Standard for Information Sciences—Permanence of Paper for
Printed Library Materials, ANSI/NISO Z39.48-1992.

Contents

Acknowledgments

We extend our appreciation to Mary Lee Danielson and George Olson for their helpful suggestions as we were planning the book and framing our ideas. We thank the following individuals for their invaluable comments and suggestions on one or more chapters: Grace Burton, Lyman Dukes III, Andrew Hayes, Larry Johnson, Gregg Jones, Judith Meece, Carol Midgett, Denise Miller, Cynthia Parshall, Rebecca Soltys, Trip Stallings, Matt Valentine, and Kin White.

Thanks are extended to Jessica Tate, Tom Tretter, and Anna Kuykendal for their work locating research documents. We appreciate the willingness of Joel Peet to share his insightful cartoons.

A number of individuals have offered their support during the writing process, and to these folks we extend our warmest appreciation: Herb Underwood, Rebecca Soltys, and Mark Hargrove.

Finally we thank all the teachers, parents, principals, central office administrators, and policy makers who have shared their perspectives with us about the consequences of high-stakes testing programs.

Introduction

The tests have affected my instruction because they have taken away the flexibility from my teaching. My kids are traditionally left out of the loop in getting to do creative activities and with the emphasis on getting the right answer on tests they are even less creative. With the emphasis on reading, writing, and arithmetic they aren't given the chance to explore and learn. It should be a fun time to learn, to wonder about the world around them, to form better critical thinking skills, and to become better human beings. My teaching has changed; I used to teach ideas rather than testing. Now I'm more focused on teaching testing stuff and if not stuff on the test, then test-taking skills like how to read a passage and decide which answer is best, or how to write an essay with a prompt. Those are skills you need, but are they the only skills you need?

(Lydia, an elementary teacher)

High-stakes testing has become the reform of choice for U. S. public schools. Politicians have increasingly used the rhetoric of accountability through testing as their primary platform for election to office. Testing has been implemented as a way to measure student achievement and school quality and as a mechanism to hold students and educators accountable. In fact, every state but Iowa has some form of high-stakes testing. This focus on testing will likely intensify, given that in January 2002, President George W. Bush signed into law the No Child Left Behind Act (2002), which calls for every child in the third through eighth grade to be tested in the basics of mathematics, reading or language arts, and (beginning in 2005) science.

But what are the unintended consequences of this type of testing? The teacher that we quoted at the beginning of this chapter identified several unintended consequences she has observed in her experiences teaching in a high-stakes testing environment. The purpose of this book is to examine the types of unintended consequences often cited by students,

1

parents, educators, and researchers. By using unintended consequences as the focus, we seek to understand how high-stakes accountability has influenced education beyond the intent of the stated policy. This book was written for educational stakeholders, including researchers, teachers, parents, administrators, and policy makers, who are interested in developing a better understanding of the complexities of testing and its effects.

HIGH-STAKES TESTS

The term "high-stakes tests" is used throughout this book to describe tests that have serious consequences for students, teachers, schools, and/or school systems. Although schools have historically used testing as a measure of student learning, testing has recently moved from being an individual student assessment to a system for ranking and comparing students. Students whose scores fail to meet established goals may be denied enrollment in particular courses, retained at a grade level until a specified score is met, or prevented from graduating.

These high-stakes tests are also used as a mechanism for public comparisons of teachers, schools, and school systems. The stakes associated with these public comparisons of schools are also high and include a variety of rewards and punishments. Schools whose students score well on tests often receive public celebrations, salary bonuses for teachers, and media recognition. On the other hand, schools that fail to meet the "standards" are provided with mandated assistance teams and receive negative media attention. In some states, low-performing schools can be taken over by the state, teachers and principals can lose their jobs, and/or teachers may be required to take competency tests to demonstrate their ability to teach.

The ideas for this book emerged from a discussion about teachers' views of high-stakes testing. It struck us as overwhelmingly peculiar that few were listening to teachers' voices in this reform debate. Collectively, we set out to listen to teachers and find ways to add their concerns, beliefs, and experiences with testing to the political rhetoric that has so far defined reform by testing.

We began our research with a statewide survey of North Carolina elementary teachers and found that their views were often in opposition to those of legislators and policy makers (Jones et al., 1999). Many teachers in Florida, Virginia, and North Carolina have reported that they believed their states' testing programs would not improve the quality of education in their schools or states (Jones, Egley, and Hogan, 2003; Jones et al., 1999; Kaplan and Owings, 2001). The media are filled with complaints about high-stakes testing, and we, too, have heard students, teachers, parents, and our colleagues state their frustrations with the new testing programs.

This is not to say that there is no support for the new testing programs. On the contrary, the public is generally in favor of the current amount of testing in the public schools (Rose and Gallup, 2001). As a result, there is a critical tension between those who support testing and those who do not. We explore the differences in these two perspectives in chapter 1.

UNINTENDED CONSEQUENCES

We believe that the reason many educators are opposed to the current form of testing programs is that many negative unintended consequences are associated with high-stakes testing. History has shown us that unintended consequences can have far-reaching impacts. For example, Einstein didn't intend to create the nuclear bomb when he formulated the theory of relativity. Nor did the person who invented Velcro foresee kindergartners disturbing a class by flipping their Velcro fasteners back and forth. In this book we examine the impact of testing on students, teachers, instructional practices, curriculum, policy, and other reform efforts. Through a careful examination of policy and practices, we describe positive and negative impacts of high-stakes testing. We also examine the implicit beliefs that underlie these growing accountability movements and the effects on children that are associated with taking an accountability perspective to reforming education.

Although we have attempted to identify *unintended* consequences of testing, it is difficult, if not impossible, to separate unintended and intended consequences. Testing programs are embedded in political agendas that are often complex, and testing policies affect a variety of stakeholders in a myriad of ways. For instance, some individuals have argued that testing systems were designed to discredit public schools by focusing on the failures of schools. They believe that this is an effort to marshal the political support needed to implement a voucher system that allows a student at one school to leave and attend another school. Indeed, this has started to happen in Florida, where (at the time of the writing of this book) about 8,900 students who attended "failing" schools were eligible to use vouchers to leave their schools and use the tax dollars spent on their public educations to pay tuition at private (and often religious) schools (Hegarty, 2002). The link between vouchers and testing has also emerged in the No Child Left Behind legislation in which students at low-performing schools will have the option to use public funds to attend a private school (U.S. Department of Education, Office of the Secretary, 2001). Is this an intended or unintended consequence of the testing system that ranked these schools low? It is not our intent in this book to describe all of the possible intended consequences. Rather, for the purposes of this book, we have assumed that the testing programs were designed to measure student achievement and school quality and to hold students and educators accountable.

OUR EVOLVING PERSPECTIVES

In this book, we look at testing through an examination of school-based research and the rich stories of those whose lives are impacted most by the testing movement. Although a number of other books describe the history of testing, the process of test construction, and philosophical stances about accountability and standards-based reform, there are limited resources that approach testing from the perspectives of teachers and principals. Therefore, we frame this book as looking from inside the classroom to the larger views of education that lie outside the classroom doors. Our backgrounds as teachers, administrators, and researchers enable us to examine the issues in new ways that have been overlooked by test designers, legislators, and politicians who are setting policy. It is our hope that when policy makers have data about the unintended consequences of the programs they are proposing, they can make more informed decisions about policy direction.

We believe that it is important for us to share our personal perspectives on testing and education, because these have undoubtedly influenced the writing of this book. As authors, our views of high-stakes testing are colored by our experiences in the public schools as students, as elementary and secondary teachers of mathematics and science, as central office administrators, and as university professors. Although we have different backgrounds, we share common beliefs about what constitutes a quality education.

We begin with a belief that schools should teach some basic skills in literacy and mathematics, where appropriate. However, these basic skills should be complemented with the teaching of strategies focused on how and when to use these skills in rich, real-world contexts. We are not opposed to students learning factual information, but we believe that passive, rote memorization of factual information should be limited. Indeed, factual knowledge is critical to becoming an expert in any field. However, factual information should be gained through meaningful learning experiences in which students are allowed to construct knowledge connected to their existing knowledge and prior life experiences. It is important to foster students' thinking skills, such as problem solving and critical thinking, to allow them to use their knowledge and skills in real-world contexts. Interdisciplinary work (such as incorporating reading and writing into a mathematics lesson) should be encouraged to promote transfer and connections to other knowledge domains.

One of our beliefs that appears to differ from traditional views of education is about the role of the teacher. We view the teacher primarily as a navigator or facilitator who *guides* students through their acquisition of knowledge and skills, as opposed to being someone who primarily *tells* students about knowledge and skills. Teachers help students tie new knowledge to their existing knowledge and help students make connections between their existing knowledge and their experiences. To this end, students should be placed in a role in which they are *active* learners who learn through hands-on and minds-on experiences. We do not advocate allowing students to have complete control of their learning; rather, we believe that teachers should structure the learning environment in a manner that promotes students' active engagement in activities that help them meet the standards.

We also find a competitive view of schooling to be incongruent with a quality education. By emphasizing collaboration among students rather than competition, we believe that more authentic environments are created that support the wide range of abilities and experiences that students bring to the learning context. In addition, we support the belief that teachers should motivate students by creating engaging learning environments and taking into consideration students' interests and abilities.

Unlike many of the loud voices heard in the media, we believe that our educational system is not broken; instead, we recognize that some schools, some classrooms, and some children have complex issues that make learning difficult. Undoubtedly, some schools need to be improved. To do so, the underlying issues must be addressed in ways that require significant investments of time and resources.

Our vision of schools is one in which students are respected; parents are informed and involved; teachers are knowledgeable, creative, and respected; and learning is an exciting endeavor that stretches beyond the classroom door. It is within these visions of teaching and learning that we examine the array of intended and unintended consequences of high-stakes testing throughout the book. We believe that it is only after society carefully considers its goals for education, coupled with all the costs of testing, that it can really decide whether high-stakes testing is an effective way to educate its students.

CHAPTER OVERVIEWS

Throughout the book, pseudonyms are used in place of teachers', administrators', and parents' names. We begin in chapter 1 with a further discussion of our perspectives on teaching and learning, along with the perspectives of proponents and opponents of testing. We then provide a brief history of schooling and testing to help readers better understand how the current testing movement came about.

In chapter 2, we discuss the consequences of high-stakes testing on the curriculum. We discuss what is meant by standards, and how testing these standards has affected *what* teachers teach. In chapter 3, we discuss the effects of testing on *how* teachers teach.

Next, in chapter 4, we examine how teachers are preparing students for tests and how this preparation has affected instruction. Moreover, we examine how test preparation can lead to negative unintended consequences such as invalidating tests, the violation of ethical practices, and an increase in cheating.

How do high-stakes tests affect students' motivation? In chapter 5, we explore this question by presenting motivational theories and discussing how these theories can provide insight into whether high-stakes testing has facilitated or hindered student motivation.

In chapter 6, we examine how testing has impacted special populations such as disabled and minority students. We explore the unintended consequences of testing on subgroups of students including ethnic minorities, children from lower socioeconomic communities, students with special learning needs, and children who do not speak English as their native language. Because testing policy does not impact all students in the same manner, we also examine the differential impacts of testing policies.

We discuss the shift in accountability from teachers to students in chapter 7 and examine the implications of social promotion. We discuss the relevant research on student retention and how high-stakes testing policies might affect students and schools in this regard.

In chapter 8, we discuss how high-stakes testing has affected teachers' job satisfaction, and as a result, how it has affected teacher retention and attrition. We describe the major factors that are associated with teacher retention and attrition and analyze how high-stakes testing affects teachers' jobs.

The language associated with testing is filled with analogies and metaphors that signal the underlying beliefs and meanings associated with accountability and education. Terms such as "standards," "performance," "high stakes," and "sanctions" bring to mind many preconceived notions of these ideas and situate assessment in the broader political agendas. In chapter 9, we take a look at different analogies that have been used for testing and how these affect how testing is viewed. By unpacking the language of testing, we show how these analogies can explain beliefs about testing while also falling short of representing the reality of schooling.

In chapter 10, we provide recommendations for educators and policy makers based on the research reviewed in this book. Then, in chapter 11, we summarize many of the key points made throughout the book and examine the effects of the unintended consequences as a whole. To do so, we compare the costs and benefits of high-stakes testing.

The purpose of this book is not to make any definitive statement on whether high-stakes testing is "good" or "bad." Rather, we present many of the unintended consequences that we have heard over and over from teachers, administrators, and researchers. We have found that the arguments made by testing proponents are often simplistic and ignore the many unintended consequences that we present in this book; we also believe that it is only through an understanding of these unintended consequences that we can begin to examine the merits and failings of high-stakes testing policies.

REFERENCES

Clinton, W. 1999. "State of the Union Address." 106th Congress, 1st Session; 106–1. Washington, D.C.: Government Printing Office.

Hegarty, S. 2002. "68 Schools Receive Failing Grade." *St. Petersburg Times*, 13 June, A1, A18.

Jones, B. D., R. Egley, and D. Hogan. 2003. "Is High Stakes Testing Right for Florida? Teachers Speak Out!" Paper presented at the annual meeting of the Eastern Educational Research Association, Hilton Head, S.C., March

Jones, M. G., D. Jones, B. Hardin, L. Chapman, T. Yarbrough, and M. Davis. 1999.

"The Impact of High-Stakes Testing on Teachers and Students." *Phi Delta Kappan* 81, no. 3 (November), 199–203.

Kaplan, L. S., and W. A. Owings. 2001. "How Principals Can Help Teachers with High-Stakes Testing: One Survey's Findings with National Implications." *NASSP Bulletin* 85, no. 622, 15–23.

National Commission on Excellence in Education. 1983. *A Nation at Risk: The Imperative for Educational Reform.* Washington, D.C.: The National Commission on Excellence in Education.

Rose, L. C., and A. M. Gallup. 2001. "The 33rd Annual Phi Delta Kappa/Gallup Poll of the Public's Attitudes toward the Public Schools." *Phi Delta Kappan* 83, no. 1, 41–58.

U.S. Department of Education, Office of the Secretary. 2001. *No Child Left Behind.* Washington, D.C.: Government Printing Office.

Chapter One

Looking through Multiple Lenses: Historical and Contemporary Perspectives of Testing

North Carolina and Florida are considered by some to be "leading" the way in education reform through high-stakes testing. As university professors in these states, we have found that individuals vary greatly in how they perceive their state's testing program. Some people strongly support it; others are vehemently against it, while others are somewhere in between these extreme opposing views. Consider one woman's viewpoint in a letter to the editor of the *St. Petersburg Times*, in which she wrote that the high-stakes testing program "is a bad program that should never have been put into practice. The teachers of Florida don't want it, the parents don't want it, the students certainly don't want it, yet we have let our state government cause incredible pain to the public school system in Florida" (Smith, 2002). In another letter to the editor, a man wrote: "Gov. Jeb Bush's FCAT program is a tremendous fraud being perpetrated on the public" (Horn, 2002). Clearly, some citizens are enraged by the testing program.

Yet in a recent poll of Americans about public education, 44 percent reported that there was "about the right amount" of emphasis on achievement testing in the public schools in their communities, and 22 percent thought there was "not enough emphasis" (Rose and Gallup, 2001). Only 31 percent of those polled thought there was "too much emphasis" on testing.

In this chapter, we describe some of the different perspectives individuals have about high-stakes testing. The perceived need for the type of high-stakes tests currently in place in many states is the result of a long

9

history of testing in the United States; therefore, we also take a look back in time to better understand the origins of the current perspectives.

PERSPECTIVES OF TESTING PROPONENTS

Proponents of testing often cite at least three major reasons why high-stakes tests are currently needed in public education: 1) to measure student achievement; 2) to provide information about the quality of schools; and 3) to hold students and educators accountable. Each of these is discussed in the sections that follow.

Students, educators, and parents need to know whether a child is learning what he or she is supposed to be learning at a given grade level. If a child is below average or is failing to achieve at grade level, then test scores can indicate whether he or she needs remediation to ensure that the child has the knowledge and skills to be successful at higher levels.

Many parents and taxpayers want to know about the quality of schools in their communities. They want to be able to discern whether schools are meeting the needs of the children, and, when individuals move to a new area, they want to be able to locate their homes in areas with high-quality schools. Furthermore, they want this information about school quality to be available in quick, intelligible, and friendly formats. Test scores are supposed to meet this need by providing public information about student achievement and indices of school quality. Lower-quality schools can be identified by their lower rankings. As one parent said, "Without high-stakes testing, how can I know how good my child's school is?"

Taxpayers want to know that their hard-earned dollars are being used wisely and that their communities are receiving quality public education programs. For politicians, the accountability aspects of high-stakes testing provide concrete evidence that funds are being used to reward successful schools and punish those schools that fail to ensure learning. For the elected official who has his or her feet "held to the fire" by taxpayers who want to know that their dollars are well spent and that their schools are of high quality, testing offers immediate reform that gives the appearance of fiscal responsibility. When organizational change is viewed from the big-picture perspective, testing by reform is quick, is relatively inexpensive, and provides legislators with significant public relations capital.

PERSPECTIVES OF TESTING
OPPONENTS

The logic behind testing proponents' premises seems clear: high-stakes tests inform the public about school quality, provide a measure of accountability, and provide information about student achievement. We believe that most reasonable citizens would agree that all of these outcomes are important. However, opponents of testing do not believe that the current testing programs achieve these outcomes. While on the surface testing appears to be a simple means to attain these outcomes, its practical implementation has proven much more difficult. In addition, many individuals view the negative consequences of testing to be greater than the positive consequences, and they reject testing on this basis.

Often the teachers, who see the consequences of the testing firsthand, are the ones most opposed to it. Two recent studies have asked teachers whether high-stakes testing was taking their state's public schools "in the right direction." In Florida, 80 percent of the 708 teachers surveyed reported that the testing program was not taking Florida's public schools in the right direction (Jones, Egley, and Hogan, 2003). In Virginia, teachers registered a similar opinion: 39 percent reported that the program was not taking schools in the right direction; 38 percent reported that they were uncertain; and 22 percent reported that the program was taking schools in the right direction (Kaplan and Owings, 2001).

Other reports indicate that parents question the integrity and accuracy of the testing and accountability programs. When a newspaper interviewed a parent who had two children in a school that had just received Florida's lowest ranking (an "F"), the parent replied: "When people look at the grade, they're going to think that the teachers are failing the students. That has absolutely not been my experience" (Gilmer, 2002, p. 6B). Another parent of a child at that school reported, "The school is an awesome school" (Gilmer, 2002, p. 6B). Obviously, an inconsistency exists between the school's test scores and the perceptions of at least two parents.

And these two parents aren't the only ones who may be confused by the assessments of schools' performance. *USA Today* found that several schools identified by the federal government as Blue Ribbon schools (an award given to excellent schools) were also identified as "failing" schools by their states (Thomas and DeBarros, 2002). "At least seven were simultaneously the nation's 'best' and 'worst' in the 2000–2001 school year; three won the exemplary title in May, just one month before the federal deadline to report failing schools" (Thomas and DeBarros, 2002, para. 5). Perhaps because the rating programs measure different aspects of school progress, the result is confusing, especially to many who do not know the criteria for each of the rating programs.

Educators have also questioned the accuracy of the tests. In North Carolina, fourth grade writing scores dropped significantly in the 2001–2002 school year after four years of increased writing scores. The North Carolina Department of Public Instruction maintained that the test was valid, but others were not as sure. One principal wrote a letter to the state superintendent stating, "My fourth-grade teachers are in an uproar about the writing test mess" (Silberman, 2002, p. 14A). A county superintendent said, "I know my schools, and I know my teachers. When I see schools drop 30 points, and I know they do a quality job of teaching writing, I've got a problem with the test" (Silberman, 2002, p. 14A). Another principal said, "It calls into question the structure of the system" (Silberman, 2002, p. 14A).

North Carolina tests fourth grade students' writing by giving them a single question (prompt) in response to which they write an essay. Because the passing rate on the 2002 test was so low, a number of educators questioned whether the prompt used for the 2002 test was appropriate. It told students: "Write a story about a time you had a great day at school" (Silberman, 2002, p. 1A). Some educators claimed that the prompt did not engage the students and encouraged students to list what happened in a manner that set them up for failure (essays receive lower scores when they have a "list-like quality"). Because of examples such as this, opponents to testing say that trying to measure a fourth grade student's writing ability through the use of one question is inappropriate and unreliable. They believe that teachers are much better at assessing students' writing because they see students' writing on a daily basis on many different topics.

The accuracy of other tests has also been questioned. As an example, the headline on the front page of the 22 May 2001 edition of *The Raleigh News & Observer* (N.C.) read: "High Passing Rate on Math Tests a Mistake, Officials Say" (Silberman, 2001, p. 1A). The article described how a grading glitch in the mathematics test allowed too many third through eighth graders to pass the test. The fact that this was not found out until after the test was given and scored raises questions as to how the passing scores are set and who decides what score is acceptable for passing.

Testing opponents would cite these types of incidents as examples of how simple test scores have failed to measure the complexity of student learning, teachers' teaching practices, and school quality. Repeatedly, educators have warned against the practice of using only one-time test scores in evaluating student progress. Moreover, testing opponents question the very notion of measuring school quality by considering only standardized test scores, because many other factors contribute to the quality of a school, such as a variety of academic courses offered; the availability of extracurricular activities; a safe environment (e.g., students do not bring guns to school, illegal drugs are not readily available); dedicated administrators, teachers, and staff; smaller class sizes; a low dropout rate; the availability of after-school programs for all students; and tutoring for at-risk students.

A BACKWARD GLANCE: THE HISTORY OF REFORM BY TESTING

At the writing of this book, the proponents of testing had succeeded in implementing high-stakes testing in every state but one. But why and how did this happen? We have already discussed several reasons why proponents perceived a need for testing. To better understand how testing came about, we provide a brief summary of some of the events leading up to the implementation of state testing on a large scale in the United States.

Early in the settlement of this country, access to education was limited to the elite. The pragmatism and instability of the American frontier was not hospitable to the development of educational systems. Great distances and poor communication combined to insulate the frontier family from the resources of the East. Assessment was more casual and often very personal, usually limited to the interaction of a single student or a small number of scholars and their teacher. The Antebellum South was in much the same condition; when a school was available, it usually took the form of an old field school, where a wealthy planter provided an itinerant teacher and a building to house the young scholars. Notable exceptions were found in the large cities, such as Charleston and Richmond. But even where the practice of schooling was most dense, it was still a small undertaking by today's standards. In many ways, schooling remained a very personal, individual process.

When Horace Mann became the secretary to the first state board of education in 1837, he attracted children to the classrooms of Massachusetts, saw to the education of teachers, supervised their continuing education, helped form the structure of what was to become an American institution, and in many ways professionalized teaching. The nineteenth century was a time of great expansion in the opportunities for formal education in the United States, but it was also the time of the most cataclysmic setbacks (during the Civil War). It was during the latter half of the nineteenth century that the tools of educational assessment were forged.

During this time, American schools began to group students by grade levels according to age. Schools began to issue progress reports that were, oftentimes, highly subjective. It was the era of the first standardized tests. The first documented achievement tests were administered in the mid-1800s as the United States began an unprecedented effort to educate the masses. From this early time in our nation's history through today, changes in American demographics have had significant impacts on educational reform and school assessments. Originally, achievement tests were intended for individual evaluation. Even in these early days of standardized testing, results were inappropriately used to compare schools and children without regard for influences not related to school (Cremin, 1964). As the United States experienced an influx of immigrants, the standardized test became a way to measure whether all children were receiving an equitable education. It became the thermostat of the "great melting pot."

Public education grew significantly following the end of World War II. This growth was reflected not only in the sheer number of students (enrollment in American high school increased by 50 percent or more during this period), but also by an unprecedented growth of curriculum expectations for schools. Schools were seen as engines for economic growth and as centers for recreational interests and community pride (Cremin, 1990). The 1960s was an era of social, cultural, and racial disruption that opened the doors for new curricula, including student choice for courses and programs of study. During the 1970s, the economy slowed; taxpayers were more reluctant to provide funds to finance the expectations they saw for public schools, expectations which had become standards against which the schools were judged. Because of the unprecedented growth and access to public schools by students with varying needs, schools were seen as offering "soft subjects," such as health, social adjustment, and recreation. At the same time, schools were under additional pressure to provide meaningful opportunities for minorities.

In 1983, the United States Department of Education's National Commission on Excellence in Education published *A Nation at Risk: The Imperative for Educational Reform*. This report was written in response to the widely held belief that the United States was at risk economically and that schools were responsible for this economic trouble. The report summarized its findings in brutal terms:

> If an unfriendly power had attempted to impose on America the mediocre educational performance that exists today, we might well have viewed it as an act of war. As it stands, we have allowed this to happen to ourselves. We have even squandered the gains in achievement made in the wake of the Sputnik challenge. Moreover, we have dismantled essential support systems which helped make these gains possible. We have, in effect, been committing an act of unthinking, unilateral educational disarmament. (U.S. Department of Education, 1983, para. 3)

This report clearly situated public education as being in crisis and in need of major reform. The report used test scores as the indicator of success and the goal of schooling. *A Nation At Risk* gave birth to an unprecedented belief in the validity of test scores as measures of quality.

According to those critical of education at the time, American education needed to be "reimagined, made more rigorous, and above all, brought under the control of experts" (Meier, 2000, p. 10). Experts were seen as those who understood the new demands of the economy, unlike educators and parents. The commission offered the following recommendations:

1. State and local high school graduation requirements [should] be strengthened, and that, at a minimum, all students seeking a diploma be required to lay the foundations in the Five New Basics [including English, math, science, social studies, and computer science].
2. Schools, colleges, and universities [should] adopt more rigorous and measurable standards, and higher expectations, for academic performance and student conduct.
3. Significantly more time [should] be devoted to learning . . . [whether it is through] more effective use of the existing school day, a longer school day, or a lengthened school year.
4. Improve the preparation of teachers . . . to make teaching a more rewarding and respected profession.
5. Citizens across the Nation [should] hold educators and elected officials responsible for providing the leadership necessary to achieve these reforms, and that citizens provide the fiscal support and stability required to bring about the reforms. (U.S. Department of Education, 1983)

The voice of business and industry during the 1980s took on new urgency as the impact of global competition was felt in terms of economic shifts and narrowing markets. Numerous reports, books, and commission findings were issued during this time.

State Focus on Testing

By 1991, the focus of school reform had shifted to the state level, and most states had instituted systems for statewide educational assessment. While there seems to have been general agreement by the states to address the achievement deficiencies stated in national reports through educational reform efforts, there was little agreement about what the specific problems were and how these problems came about. Was it an outgrowth of educational bureaucracy, poor teacher training strategies, an emphasis on lower-level achievement goals, economic disparities between school systems or families? Or did the fault lie in social and cultural conditions that deprived students of opportunities to achieve appropriately?

Great emphasis was placed on statewide testing during the 1990s as a means of determining academic achievement status. During the 1994–1995 school year, only seven states did not conduct any statewide educational assessment in grades kindergarten through fifth grade (Bond and Braskamp, 1996). Of the forty-three states with testing programs, sixteen had programs that primarily focused on the three Rs—reading (including language arts), writing, and math. By 2000, all states except Iowa administered their own statewide tests.

While nearly 85 percent of states used multiple-choice exams for statewide assessments, most also combined these with other forms of performance assessment. During the 1993–1994 school year, thirty-eight states assessed writing, twenty-five states used other performance assessments, and seven states required portfolios. Two states, Kentucky and Maine, had abandoned multiple-choice testing altogether in favor of alternative assessment strategies (Bond and Braskamp, 1996). However, Maine and Kentucky have since returned to using multiple-choice tests, and standardized tests remain the rule of the day due to the excessive cost of other forms of assessment.

A study by the United States General Accounting Office predicted that a national multiple-choice achievement test would cost about 40 million dollars, while a slightly longer test with short performance-based questions would cost 210 million dollars. According to a 1993 estimate, statewide performance assessments would cost thirty-five to seventy dol-

lars per student, whereas standardized multiple-choice tests can cost as little as one to two dollars per student (United States General Accounting Office, 1993).

As the 1990s drew to a close, forty-three states used assessment as their goal for improving instruction; forty-one states used this information for performance reporting. Other purposes for assessment included program evaluation (thirty-seven states), student diagnosis (twenty-six states), high school graduation (seventeen states), and school accreditation (twelve states). In almost half of the schools studied, stakes associated with testing were high and included funding gains and losses, loss of accreditation, warnings, and eventual state takeover of schools (Caudell, 1996).

No Child Left Behind

President George Bush's 2002 No Child Left Behind legislation mandated annual state assessments of students in grades three through eight in reading and mathematics. This testing policy requires that schools "must have clear, measurable goals focused on basic skills and essential knowledge" (United States Department of Education, 2002). Furthermore, it states that if a school is identified as low-performing and fails to improve for three years, disadvantaged students should be allowed to use federal funds to attend other public or private schools of their choice. According to the policy, the driving force behind the new law was to ensure that schools are accountable for the funds they receive from the government.

The No Child Left Behind legislation represents a major shift in policy, taking accountability out of the hands of local and state governments and placing it firmly in the control of the federal government, at an estimated cost of 2 billion dollars (Kiely and Henry, 2001). A close look at the legislation shows the political realities of this point in time. The policy places value on rewards and sanctions and spells out the costs of failing to meet these guidelines. A significant shift toward school choice will allow public dollars to be used for private education. The bill defines educational quality in terms of achievement scores, clearly delineating the link between scores and educational value. In addition, the bill calls for the introduction of character education into the curriculum as well as for "rescuing victims of school-based crimes" from unsafe schools by allowing them to attend other schools.

Although the rhetoric of No Child Left Behind seems to be a worthy goal, a close look at the politics of this reform effort shows a more narrow view of educational change. This legislation allows parents and students to leave schools that have problems and use public funds to attend private schools. But although the provision for allowing crime victims to leave unsafe schools may protect a victim, the bill does little to address the underlying issues that led to school violence, poverty, or low achievement. The basic premise of this bill appears to rest on the notion that schools will either get better quickly, or they will go out of business for lack of "customers." This economics-based model reflects the business perspectives of the creators of this legislation. Although the goal of providing a quality education to every child is desirable, the option to simply abandon public schools fails to recognize the critical role a strong public education plays in a democratic society.

FINAL COMMENTS

A myriad of high-stakes assessment programs at all levels of government have swept through the American educational agenda at a speed that leaves many educators breathless. Through an examination of the historical contexts of the American educational system, the roots of the accountability initiatives can be understood within the prevailing beliefs about the purposes of schooling and the politics of reform movements. Testing in American history has passed through many stages, from its early beginnings as a more personal means of measuring individual achievement to a means of measuring the quality of schools and providing student and educator accountability.

Many educators are aware of how quickly past educational reforms have come and gone and are likely waiting to see how long the current one will last. Aware of past fleeting policies, policy makers and state departments of education appear even more resolved to stay the course this time and continue on with high-stakes testing programs. For this reason, it is important to understand the unintended consequences of these programs. The next chapter discusses how testing has affected various aspects of the curriculum.

REFERENCES

Bond, L. A., and D. Braskamp. 1996. *The Status Report of the Assessment Programs in the United States: State Student Assessment Programs Database School Year 1994–1995*. ERIC Document Reproduction Service No. ED 401 333.

Caudell, L. S. 1996. "High Stakes Innovation Meets Backlash as States Struggle with Large-Scale Assessment." *Northwest Education* 2, no. 1, 26–28, 35.

Cremin, L. 1964. *The Transformation of the School: Progressivism in American Education 1876–1957*. New York: Vintage Books.

Cremin, L. 1990. *Popular Education and Its Discontents*. New York: Harper and Row.

Florida Department of Education. 2001. *Keys to FCAT: Information about the 2002 Test, State of Florida*.

Gilmer, K. R. 2002. "48 A's . . . and Two F's." *St. Petersburg Times*, 13 June, 1B, 6B.

Horn, A. 2002. "A Tremendous Fraud" (Letter to the Editor). *St. Petersburg Times*, 18 June, 7A.

Jones, B. D., R. Egley, and D. Hogan. 2003. "Is High Stakes Testing Right for Florida? Teachers Speak Out!" Paper to be presented at the annual meeting of the Eastern Educational Research Association, Hilton Head, S.C., 26 February–4 March.

Kaplan, L. S., and W. A. Owings. 2001. "How Principals Can Help Teachers with High-Stakes Testing: One Survey's Findings with National Implications." *NASSP Bulletin* 85, no. 622, 15–23.

Kiely, K., and T. Henry. 2001. "Will No Child Be Left Behind?" *USA Today*, 17 December, D4.

Meier, D. 2000. *Educating a Democracy: Standards and the Future of Public Education*. Boston: Beacon Press.

Rose, L. C., and A. M. Gallup. 2001. "Phi Delta Kappa/Gallup Poll of the Public's Attitudes toward the Public Schools." *Phi Delta Kappan* 83, no. 1, 41–58.

Silberman, T. 2001. "High Passing Rate on Math Tests a Mistake, Officials Say." *Raleigh (N.C.) News & Observer*, 22 May, 1A, 10A.

Silberman, T. 2002. "Writing Scores Tumble." *Raleigh (N.C.) News & Observer*, 8 June, 1A, 14A.

Smith, B. S. 2002. "An Undeserved Humiliation" (Letter to the Editor). *St. Petersburg Times*, 18 June, 7A.

Thomas, K., and A. DeBarros. 2002. "School 'Excellence' Thrown a Grading Curve." www.usatoday.com/news/education/2002–08–04-schools-usat_x.htm (accessed 17 August 2002).

United States Department of Education, National Commission on Excellence in Education. 1983. *A Nation at Risk: The Imperative for Educational Reform*. Washington, D.C.: Author.

United States Department of Education. 2002. *Executive Summary: No Child Left Behind*. www.ed.gov/inits/ncib/part2.html (accessed 15 July 2002).

United States General Accounting Office. 1993. *Educational Achievement Standards: NAGB's Approach Yields Misleading Interpretations*. Washington, D.C.: Author.

Chapter Two

How Testing Shapes the Curriculum

At Sanders Elementary School in North Carolina, the principal and faculty work together to create a curriculum that is developmentally appropriate for children; involves teaching for understanding; is learner-centered; and strives to give all children access to culturally rich experiences with art, music, dance, and history. The school is working toward heterogeneous grouping of students, with a special emphasis on inclusion of children with special needs in the regular classroom. There is a science laboratory where children go for science instruction offered by a specialist. Children often stop by the science lab each morning to greet the rabbit and help feed the fish. Each year, the entire fifth grade goes to a nearby nursing home to visit with the elderly and share songs. Parents come into the school on a regular basis to talk about their careers in medicine, law enforcement, and business. Recognizing the need for intense, early intervention with young children, teachers in first, second, and third grades have a teacher assistant to ensure that all children get a good start on their education. The school enjoys a special place in the community, and the principal and teachers generally enjoy working together to meet the needs of all their students.

Two years later, following the introduction of high-stakes testing, this school is a different place. The initial test scores were moderately low, because, according to the teachers, the test didn't measure what they taught. The school's achievement-based ranking was announced simultaneously to the principal and press. The principal was told that scores must go up or he would lose his job and the school could be taken over by the state. Now, the science lab has been closed, and the money that went for science kits is used to purchase test preparation booklets. The special education inclusion teacher's position has been shifted to a literacy position for someone to tutor children throughout the school whose test scores were low. Teacher assistants have been reassigned to work with upper-grade classes to improve test scores. Although the principal strongly supported the visits to the nursing home, all of the fifth grade teachers voted not to go, and instead, they used the time to prepare students for the tests. Teacher morale has suffered, and teachers look suspiciously at each other as they wonder who is bringing the scores down. Essentially, all of the assemblies, field trips, and parent career talks have been stopped in order to focus on teaching reading, writing, and mathematics. The teachers of special subjects fight with the regular classroom teachers for time for the children to come to music, art, and physical education. Although children still go to these classes, they go much less frequently than before, and all special teachers are reassigned to regular classrooms where they tutor children whose scores are low. At the end of the year, the scores go up in reading, writing, and mathematics. The teachers and principal have decided to continue their focus on these subjects to make sure their scores don't drop. But in their hearts and minds, there is conflict over whether or not this is the right thing to do.

Although Sanders Elementary is a fictitious school, every single one of the changes that were described for this school have been documented as schools in a single school system coped with high-stakes assessment (Danielson, 1999). Deciding what gets taught in a limited school day is a tough decision. On one hand, one wonders what good it does a child to learn about careers, visit a nursing home, or participate in a school play if he or she can't read, write, or do mathematics. Alternatively, what good does having basic skills do a child whose life is missing the richness of culture, music, art, and relationships with adults in the community?

These essential questions about what should be taught in schools have led to some of the greatest controversies in education. The question of what should be in the curriculum stirs hot debates, ranging from what books should be found in a middle school library to whether or not evolution should be included in biology classes. Perspectives on school curricula are rooted in religious and political values, as well as in a wide range of agendas of special interest groups. Views differ from community to community, sometimes with wide disagreements held by people according to region and state. Even the issue of states' rights enters into school curricula, as people debate on having local, state, or national curricula.

Part of the support for high-stakes testing emerges from conservatives who typically seek a traditional education for their children. For many, the goal of schooling is the transmission of knowledge. According to this perspective, an educated citizenry is one that can show mastery of a body of knowledge. This view of schooling places authority in written text and values a command of the "material." For many Americans, this transmission view of learning formed the basis of their own educations and it follows that what worked for them should be good enough for their children. This type of curriculum brings to mind comforting notions of the historical one-room schoolhouse and of children learning reading, writing, and arithmetic. It feels safe, homey, and simple. Without question, students need to know essential information and possess fundamental skills, but the reality of our world today and the future world of our children calls for a different type of education, one grounded in an ability to use information in applications only dreamed about in our parents' time.

Modern technological advancements have rendered the notion of education as mere mastery of information relatively useless. Knowledge is being generated and shared at massive levels never seen before in human history. For the first time ever, information is available through the Internet to anyone, no matter where they are in the world. For the future citizens, the goal isn't going to lie in what they can remember, but rather in their ability to locate information and use it in ways that make it meaningful. As education moves from a look backward to a look forward, assessment has been caught between these worlds of differences. Many of the assessments that currently compose high-stakes testing measure only the amount of knowledge, and not the student's skill in using this knowledge. In a study of six major standardized tests and tests associated with four major textbooks in mathematics and science, researchers found that published tests failed to measure the higher-order thinking skills and topics that teachers felt were important (Madaus et al., 1992).

As we Americans define and redefine the curricula of our schools, we are left with critical tensions between the need to teach basic knowledge and the more complex skills needed to use and apply knowledge. Furthermore, how should we define standards or competencies that all students should have, given the rapidly changing nature of our society?

WHOSE CURRICULUM STANDARDS?

"Raising standards" has emerged as the catchphrase of the accountability movement. Policy makers implement high-stakes testing in an effort to "raise standards." But there is a huge gap in the meaning of the term "standards" as it is used by educators as opposed to politicians. The misunderstandings about the claimed use of "standards" have set the reform of education back considerably. "Standards," to professional educators, means a vision of teaching and learning in which students are engaged in high-level conceptual learning. But the term "standards," as used within the accountability movement, generally implies basic skills. Thompson (2001) calls the two uses of the term "standards" the case of the evil twin. According to Thompson, "[i]n the case of the standards movement, the evil twin [of the accountability movement] is the more visible and powerful of the siblings and so its authentic namesake [of professional education] is in an increasingly perilous situation" (p. 358).

Educators have been working on developing comprehensive standards for teaching, assessment, professional development, and curriculum since the 1980s. The first standards document was *Curriculum and Evaluation Standards for School Mathematics* produced by the National Council of Teachers of Mathematics (NCTM)(1989). Teachers, administrators, mathematics educators, and mathematicians developed the mathematics standards through a process that involved lengthy discussions about what a student should know and be able to do. The draft of the emerging document was reviewed by the larger educational community, and the NCTM still maintains an ongoing revision process. The mathematics standards have served as a vision of quality mathematics instruction, providing direction for curriculum development, teacher professional development, and instructional practices.

Following the mathematics standards, the science education community developed two standards documents that have served as a road map for educational reform. The American Association for the Advancement of Science (AAAS) developed the *Benchmarks for Science Literacy* (1993), which were built on research about how students develop understandings of science phenomena as well as on defining and sequencing science content. The *Benchmarks* discuss key ideas and themes that cut across the disciplines of science. Instead of a typical assessment standard, such as "The sixth grade student will be able to name the three states of matter," the *Benchmarks* describe how students develop understandings of states of matter and what topics should be taught before and after in order for students to develop deeper understandings. The *Benchmarks* suggest grade ranges (rather than single grades) for teaching content, recognizing that students develop along a continuum. Science educators and teachers have welcomed the *Benchmarks* as a document that accurately reflects the complexity of teaching science to students who bring a wide range of prior experiences and understandings to the classroom. The document encourages a long-range view of the development of phenomena.

These views of standards by professional educators and content experts contrast sharply with the standards that are discussed by politicians with regard to testing. The typical high-stakes testing standard advocated by politicians seeks to have students master the traditional "basic skills" of reading, writing, and mathematics.

Table 2.1 shows some of the fundamental differences in testing standards and professional standards. Although there are assessments such as portfolios and performance-based assessments that reflect the fundamental beliefs of professional standards, the typical high-stakes test falls under the description of testing standards. The differences in the philosophical underpinnings of these views of standards are large and contribute to the negative perspectives that many teachers have of high-stakes testing. Professional standards are based on beliefs of the uniqueness of children and recognition of the wide variation of skills, knowledge, and experiences that they possess. Furthermore, professional standards are built upon a vision of excellence in teaching that promotes learning in meaningful and authentic contexts. On the other hand, reform by testing focuses on achievement, mastery, and competency. Testing necessitates approaches that call for all students of a single grade to master a common set of skills and knowledge. Testing standards mandate that these outcomes of instruction be clearly and easily measurable. Politicians who oversee testing standards ensure that standards are quickly imple-

Table 2.1 Testing Standards and Professional Standards

Testing Standards	Professional Standards
Designate what all children will do at a grade level	Outline conceptual understandings across grade levels
Created by psychometricians	Created by content experts, parents, teachers, and community members
Written in testable terminology	Written as broad concepts
Tightly sequenced	Broadly sequenced
Staff development geared toward test scores	Staff development geared toward instruction
Instruction for mastery	Instruction for conceptual understanding
Single measure of competency	Multiple measures of competency
Focused	Pluralistic
Isolates learning from the cultural context	Embeds learning in cultural contexts
Goal is achievement	Goal is learning

mented and are designed to measure immediate change in students' knowledge. The reality of short political lives means that politicians need test scores to go up before the next election. The testing standards dictate a curriculum that is simple, easy to measure, with limitations on ambiguity and complex interpretations. In contrast, teachers value a curriculum that authentically incorporates this same complexity into instruction.

WHOSE KNOWLEDGE COUNTS?

Testing sharply defines the knowledge and skills that students will learn. But who makes the decisions about what knowledge is considered critical? Prior to high-stakes testing, teachers made the decision about what to teach within a broad framework of topics. Testing, however, not only defines what will be taught, but also defines the context of the knowledge. Whereas teachers may have previously embedded instruction in integrated units or taught concepts across multiple grades, testing necessitates that topics be taught in ways that can be assessed through discrete items on written tests given at very specific points of time. Research on students' conceptual ecologies has shown that students' knowledge isn't typically isolated in memory, but instead is richly connected to related concepts and prior experiences (cf. Carey, 1991; Jones, Carter, and Rua, 1999). Many high-stakes assessments ask students to strip away the richness of their knowledge as they struggle to answer discrete test items that have a single correct response.

State and local curricular frameworks are typically developed through a process that involves parents, teachers, content experts, and community members. But tests are typically developed by psychometricians and commercial testing businesses that are distanced from the day-to-day world of the classroom teacher. This question of who defines what is tested, and more importantly, what is taught, is perhaps the most critical issue to confront schools. Historically, curricula have supported the dominant cultural group to the exclusion of the perspectives and views of minority groups. (For example, teaching children that Columbus discovered the Americas ignores the fact that there were native peoples in the Americas long before the Europeans arrived.) The current testing movement has been accused of maintaining the power structure of the dominant culture.

> It is not coincidental that the concerted effort by government authorities to gain monopoly control over the curriculum (through testing) arrives at the time

that social movements have appeared and are challenging male, White Anglo-European political and cultural supremacy. The formerly enslaved, colonized, and oppressed do not accept their ascribed cultural, racial, and gender inferiority. Many are asserting their rights to reclaim cultural power, and to create and forge their own cultural and social identities. (Berlak, 2000, p. 94)

Bill Bigelow, an Oregon social studies teacher, believes that the testing movement is an attempt to shut down efforts by educators to create a pluralistic society that values cultural diversity (Bigelow, 2000). According to Bigelow, the narrow definition of what is taught leads to a conservative, "father knows best" view of curriculum. Bigelow describes the Oregon social studies test:

A typical 49-question high-school field test piloted in 1998 included seven questions on global climate, two on the location of rivers in India and Africa, and one on hypothetical world population projections in the year 2050. But not a single question in the test concerned the lives of people around the world, or environmental conditions—nothing about increasing poverty, the global AIDS epidemic, disappearance of the rain forests, rates of unemployment, global warming, etc., or efforts to address these crises. The test bounced aimlessly from one disjointed fact to another. In the most profound sense it was pointless. (Bigelow, 2000)

This teacher's comment reflects the discomfort that teachers have with external testing that seems disconnected to the complexity of curriculum issues and perspectives. Furthermore, this social studies teacher highlights the tension that is created when we use tests in high-stakes situations. Statewide testing programs are limited in what can be tested reliability and validly. As we discuss in the sections that follow, the disconnect between the rich curriculum of the classroom and the mandated, tested curriculum is a common and difficult problem to resolve.

CURRICULUM REFORM THROUGH TESTING

The curriculum, in the narrow sense, is typically defined as a written description of what students will learn in a particular grade or course. Curricula often exist simultaneously at a variety of different levels including the school, the district, the state, and professional organizations. But the curriculum often includes much more than the outline of topics that are included in instruction; it also includes aspects of student development, sequencing of content and skills, applications of learning, student activities, and the organization of instruction. There is also the larger context of the enacted curriculum that goes beyond written educational objectives to include the lived experiences of teachers and students in individual classrooms (Snyder, Bolin, and Zumwalt, 1992). Teachers often include a myriad of topics and skills in their instruction that are in addition to the formal written curriculum. This distinction between what is prescribed and what is enacted is important as we look at how high-stakes testing influences what teachers choose to teach and how they structure valuable educational time.

From the perspective of policy makers, high-stakes testing is designed to ensure that teachers will align their curriculum with the content of the state test (Popham et al., 1985). This type of measurement-driven reform (Popham et al., 1985) is accomplished through the accompanying high stakes such as public announcements of school scores, financial incentives, the threat of job loss, and potential school takeover by the state. But measurement-driven reform is based on the belief that assessments can accurately measure learning. The validity of tests comes into question with studies such as the one by Koretz, Linn, and Shepard (1991), which found that when students were tested with a second test that was equivalent to the school system's mathematics test, students performed much worse on the new test than they did on the school system test, even though the tests measured the same content and skills. It isn't clear why student performance varied in this study, but if two tests are equivalent, they should yield the same results.

THE IMPACT OF TESTING ON SUBJECTS TESTED

When testing emphasizes areas that are not part of the traditional curriculum, there is evidence that teachers shift their instruction to increase emphasis on the tested areas (Corbett and Wilson, 1991; McNeil, 2000). Firestone et al. (2001) studied the specific areas that mathematics teachers teach and found that when testing emphasized operations with fractions, measurement, and probability, teachers shifted their instruction away from computation and increased time spent on fractions, statistics, and patterns and functions. Furthermore, the study found that instructional time was being spread broadly across a number of new topics, without a focus on any area. Firestone et al. (2001) believed their data supported the criticism that the American curriculum has little depth and that teachers tend to cover short segments of topics over and over again without depth in any area (Schmidt, McKnight, and Raizen, 1996). Other research on high-stakes testing shows that testing causes teachers to carefully align their instruction with the official curriculum that is tested. As described further below, what gets tested gets taught. In this sense, reform through testing is successful. If the goal is to improve achievement in reading, writing, and mathematics (as in the original assessment programs of North Carolina and Florida), then testing only these subjects creates an instructional focus, and if the stakes are high enough, schools will spend their time, energy, and resources on the tested topics.

THE IMPACT ON TESTING ON SUBJECTS NOT TESTED

The downside of high-stakes testing in only a few subjects is the dramatic impact the policy has on nontested subjects. In our study of North Carolina elementary teachers' views of the impact of high-stakes testing, teachers reported that after the implementation of the testing program, they spent substantially more time teaching the tested subjects of mathematics, reading, and writing and less time teaching science, social studies, the arts, and physical education and health (Jones et al., 1999). This stratified, random sample survey of 236 teachers found that on average, teachers spent the most time each week teaching reading (401 minutes per week), followed by mathematics (292 minutes) and writing (198 minutes). The nontested subjects were taught on average much less frequently. Social studies was taught for only 102 minutes, science 99 minutes, music and health about 44 minutes each, and physical education only 61 minutes. The teachers were asked if these time allocations were the same as in years prior to testing, and 67 percent said they were spending more time on reading, 65 percent said they were spending more time on writing, and 56 percent said they were spending more time teaching mathematics each week. This narrowing of the curriculum has been reported in virtually every state where there is high-stakes testing of only a few subjects (cf. Borko and Stecher, 2001; Jones and Johnston, 2002).

When the majority of instructional time is dedicated to a few tested topics, the rest of the time becomes a fought-over commodity. The leftover subjects are moved, removed, and reduced as schools struggle with an overloaded school day. How do teachers and principals decide what has value and what doesn't? In response to the narrow testing of only a few subjects, a Virginia superintendent said she was considering moving the arts to a weekend program, doing away with vocational education, and having physical education become an independent study subject in which students would sign pledges that they had engaged in physical activity to prepare themselves for the President's Physical Fitness Test (Hess and Brigham, 2000). For this superintendent, the goal of increasing test scores influenced her decisions about curricular content and balance.

Whereas a state such as Texas may decide subjects like science are basic and therefore are included in statewide assessments, other states like Florida or North Carolina have not historically included science in the definition of basics. As a result, subjects like science are either not taught or the time for their instruction is reduced (Jones and Johnston, 2002).

The Shifting Sands of Different Tests

Firestone et al. (2001) studied mathematics and science instruction in relation to statewide testing in New Jersey and found that testing can differentially impact curricular areas. This study found that when science testing was initially introduced, teachers increased the amount of time they spent teaching a variety of science topics. However, when the testing results showed that students were scoring as more proficient in science than in mathematics and language arts, the curriculum shifted away from science instruction toward the areas where scores were poorer. On the surface, this shift toward spending time helping students with areas that need improvement makes sense. But looking a little deeper, we ask what the test scores really measure, who set the performance levels and why, and whether teachers should quit teaching areas of the curriculum in which students do well (at least as measured by the test).

In Illinois, teachers find that the science test tends to measure content knowledge to the exclusion of the process skills. As a result of this perception, teachers have shaped their instruction to match the knowledge focus of the science test (Barker, 2001), a change that is in opposition to recent science education reform recommendations that call for the teaching of science process skills.

TESTING AND YOUNG CHILDREN

Teachers recognize that children vary widely in their cognitive, social, and emotional development. The notion of testing all first graders in March with a single test to measure achievement ignores the wide variation in development and seems absurd to experienced teachers. Educators have long recognized that age is only roughly correlated with development. Practices such as multiage grouping reflect this recognition of the variation in children. For most teachers, being asked to gloss over the variations in children's development and to teach all of them the same content at the same time is asking them to violate their fundamental beliefs about best instructional practice.

But one has to ask, have we been expecting too little from children in the name of delayed development? Have expectations in public schools been high enough to maximize children's learning? For many in public sectors, the answer is clearly no. There are teachers, schools, and school districts that, for a variety of reasons, have held low expectations for children. But these are schools where neither professional standards nor testing standards are being implemented, and typically these are schools troubled by serious and complex issues such as poverty, large cultural disparities, and/or a lack of effective leadership. What is needed is a closer look at these schools to address issues of poverty and leadership simultaneously with a challenging curriculum that not only teaches essential skills but also teaches critical thinking and problem solving.

One of the unintended consequences of high-stakes testing is the loss of developmentally appropriate instruction. Although high-stakes assessments started with high school competency tests, testing programs have moved down through the grades as schools attempt to identify and help children who are having academic difficulty earlier and earlier. In grades K–3, "reform by testing" movements have conflicted with early childhood educators' commitment to developmentally appropriate practices.

The National Association for the Education of Young Children (NAEYC) has worked for years to promote instructional practices that reflect what we know about how children grow and develop. See box 2.1 for an excerpt about their position regarding issues related to testing. NAEYC's recommendations for young children reflect NAEYC's commitment to children by respecting the dignity, worth, and uniqueness of each individual. NAEYC's developmentally appropriate practice states: "When individual children do not make expected learning progress, neither grade retention nor social promotion are used; instead, initiatives such as more focused time, individualized instruction, tutoring, or other individual strategies are used to accelerate children's learning" and "[e]arly childhood programs use multiple indicators of progress in all development domains to evaluate the effect of the program on children's development and learning and regularly report children's progress to parents. Group-administered, standardized, multiple-choice achievement tests are not used before third grade, preferably not before fourth grade" (NAEYC, 1996, p. 1).

In spite of NAEYC's policy, schools are submitting to pressure to test children earlier and earlier. According to Steven Ballowe, deputy superintendent for curriculum and instruction in Beaufort County, South Carolina, testing can retard developmentally appropriate practices: "We had to wean teachers away from the old practices (before developmentally appropriate instruction)" (Harrington-Lueker, 2000, p. 1). But now, according to Ballowe, teachers are returning to their old routines to prepare for the tests. Increasingly, early childhood experts say that in order to prepare for tests, "schools . . . downplay exploration, hands-on learning and a flexible curriculum and instead drill students in specific, structured academic content" (Harrington-Lueker, 2000, p. 2).

In sum, an unintended consequence of high-stakes testing policy is a loss of developmentally appropriate practices for young children.

Box 2.1: Testing Position Statement from the National Association for the Education of Young Children

The practice of administering standardized tests to young children has increased dramatically in recent years. . . . [M]ore and more 5- and 6-year-olds are denied admission to school or are assigned to some form of extra year tracking, such as "developmental kindergarten," retention in kindergarten, or "transitional" first grade. . . . Such practices (often based on inappropriate uses of readiness or screening test) disregard the potential, documented long-term negative effects of retention on children's self-esteem and the fact that such practices disproportionately affect low-income and minority children; further, these practices have been implemented in the absence of research documenting they positively affect children's later academic achievement. . . .

The negative influence of standardized testing on the curriculum is not limited to kindergarten. Throughout the primary grades, schools assess achievement using tests that frequently do not reflect current theory and research about how children learn. . . . Too many school systems teach to the test or continue to use outdated instructional methods so that children will perform adequately on standardized tests. The widespread use of standardized tests also drains resources of time and funds without clear demonstration that the investment is beneficial to children.

Ironically, the calls for excellence in education that have produced widespread reliance on standardized testing may have had the opposite effect—mediocrity. Children are being taught to provide one "right" answer on the answer sheet, but are not being challenged to think. Rather than producing excellence, the overuse (and misuse) of standardized testing has led to the adoption of inappropriate teaching practices as well as admission and retention policies that are not in the best interest of individual children or the nation as a whole. (National Association for the Education of Young Children, 1987, p. 1)

POLITICS OF CURRICULUM CHANGE

Another consequence of high-stakes testing is teachers' loss of control over the curriculum. Smith (1991), in a study of test preparation practices of Arizona teachers, found that administrators used testing as a way to control what teachers taught and how they taught it. As Smith noted: "Because ends and means are dependent, controlling what must be attained on standard measures effectively controls what must be taught and by what methods" (Smith, 1991, pp. 539–40). The battles about high-stakes testing are at the core a battle of control over what is taught, by whom, and how it is taught. Where once the teacher was the sole person who decided the curriculum, high-stakes testing puts that control firmly in the hands of politicians. This shift in power, respect, and professional autonomy leaves teachers caught between their beliefs in best practices and their need to show those in power what their students know and can do. For others, this shift in power represents a type of social engineering that "[e]mpowers a small group of education bureaucrats, operating largely in secret without public accountability, to manipulate testing results to achieve any number of social or educational ends" (Malhoit, 2001, p. 13A). For the teacher in the classroom who must face the public scrutiny of test scores, altering the curriculum is one way of gaining some measure of control over externally mandated testing policies for which he or she has little control.

Of all the consequences of high-stakes testing, the impact of testing on the curriculum is perhaps the most dramatic. Testing policy is designed to ensure that teachers are covering the curriculum established at each grade level and to ensure that each child's achievement grows by at least a grade level per year. However, the types of changes that take place with high-stakes testing are much more dramatic than asking teachers to address the grade-level curriculum. As we have discussed in this chapter, teachers have abandoned or reduced their instruction in art, music, science, and social studies. Early grade teachers have begun to move away from community service projects and developmentally appropriate practices as they gear their students up to participate in testing programs. Even the enacted curriculum within classes changes from a professional standards-based curriculum that focuses on conceptual understanding and problem solving to a modified curriculum that reflects the narrower types of information included on standardized tests. Furthermore, the alteration of the curriculum that accompanies testing programs is done without public discussion and professional debate about the content of our nation's instructional programs. Although testing policy is designed to take the "fluff" out of the instructional day and promote the instruction of the designated curriculum, eliminating visits to nursing homes, reducing science instruction, and cutting off music and art classes in schools is clearly an unintended consequence of high-stakes testing.

REFERENCES

American Association for the Advancement of Science. 1993. *Benchmarks for Science Literacy.* New York: Oxford University Press.

Barker, H. 2001. "Between the Culture of Change and the Culture of Testing: Negotiating a Space to Teach Science." Paper presented at the annual meeting of the National Association of Research in Science Teaching, St. Louis, Mo., 25–28 March.

Berlak, B. 2000. "Standards and the Control of Knowledge." In *Failing Our Kids: Why the Testing Craze Won't Fix Our Schools*, ed. K. Swope and B. Minor, 93–94. Milwaukee, Wisc.: Rethinking Schools, Ltd.

Bigelow, B. 2000. "Standards and Multiculturalism." In *Failing Our Kids: Why the Testing Craze Won't Fix Our Schools*, ed. K. Swope and B. Minor, 87–92. Milwaukee, Wisc.: Rethinking Schools, Ltd.

Borko, H., and B. Stecher. 2001. "Looking at Reform through Different Methodological Lenses: Surveys and Case Studies of the Washington State Educational Reform." Paper presented at the American Educational Research Association Conference, Seattle, Wash., 11 April.

Carey, S. 1991. "Knowledge Acquisition: Enrichment or Conceptual Change?" In *The Epigenesis of Mind: Essays on Biology and Cognition*, ed. S. Carey and R. Gelman, 257–91. Hillsdale, N.J.: Erlbaum.

Corbett, H. D., and B. L. Wilson. 1991. *Testing, Reform, and Rebellion.* Norwood, N.J.: Ablex.

Danielson, M. L. 1999. *How Principals Perceive and Respond to a High Stakes Accountability Measure.* Unpublished dissertation, University of North Carolina at Chapel Hill.

Firestone, W., L. Monfils, G. Camilli, R. Schorr, J. Hicks, and D. Mayrowetz. 2001. "The Ambiguity of Test Preparation: A Multimethod Analysis in One State." Paper presented at the annual meeting of the American Educational Research Association, Seattle, Wash., 11 April.

Harrington-Lueker, D. 2000. "The Uneasy Coexistence of High Stakes and Developmentally Appropriate Practice." *The School Administrator* 57, no. 10. www.aasa.org/publications/sa/2000_01/harrington.htm (accessed 11 April 2002).

Hess, F. M., and F. Brigham. 2000. "None of the Above: The Promise and Peril of High Stakes Testing." *American School Board Journal* 187, no. 1, 26–29.

Jones, M. G., G. Carter, and M. Rua. 1999. "Exploring the Development of Conceptual Ecologies: Communities of Concepts Related to Convection and Heat." *Journal of Research in Science Teaching* 37, 139–59.

Jones, B. D., and A. F. Johnston. 2002. "The Effects of High-Stakes Testing on

Instructional Practices." Paper presented at the 2002 annual meeting of the American Educational Research Association, New Orleans, La., April.

Jones, M. G., D. Jones, B. Hardin, L. Chapman, T. Yarbrough, and M. Davis. 1999. "The Impact of High Stakes Testing on Teachers and Students." *Phi Delta Kappan* 81, no. 3 (November), 199–203.

Koretz, D. M., R. L. Linn, and L. A. Shepard. 1991. "The Effects of High-Stakes Testing on Achievement: Preliminary Findings about Generalization across Tests." Paper presented at the annual meeting of the American Educational Research Association, Chicago, April.

Madaus, G. F., M. M. West, M. Harmon, R. G. Lomax, and K. A. Viator. 1992. *The Influence of Testing on Teaching Math and Science in Grades 4–12: Appendix D: Testing and Teaching in Six Urban Sites.* Chestnut Hill, Mass.: Center for the Study of Testing, Evaluation, and Educational Policy, Boston College.

Malhoit, G. 2001. "Manipulation Rules the System." *Raleigh (N.C.) News and Observer,* 5 July, 13A.

McNeil, L. 2000. *Contradictions of School Reform: Educational Costs of Standardized Testing.* New York: Routledge.

National Association for the Education of Young Children. 1987. *Standardized Testing of Young Children 3 through 8 Years of Age.* Policy statement. www.naeyc.org/resources/position_statements/pstestin.htm (accessed 11 April 2002).

National Association for the Education of Young Children. 1996. *Policies Essential for Achieving Developmentally Appropriate Practice in Early Childhood Programs: Developmentally Appropriate Practice in Early Childhood Programs Serving Children from Birth through Age 8.* Policy statement. www.naeyc.org/resources/position_statements/dap6.htm (accessed 11 April 2002).

National Council of Teachers of Mathematics. 1989. *Curriculum and Evaluation Standards for School Mathematics.* Reston, Va: Author.

Popham, J., K. Cruse, S. Rankin, P. Sandifer, and P. Williams. 1985. "Measurement-Driven Instruction: It's on the Road." *Phi Delta Kappan* 66, 628–35.

Schmidt, W. H., C. C. McKnight, and S. A. Raizen. 1996. *A Splintered Vision: An Investigation of U.S. Science and Mathematics Education.* East Lansing, Mich.: U.S. National Research Center for the Third International Mathematics and Science Study.

Smith, M. L. 1991. "Meanings of Test Preparation." *American Educational Research Journal* 28, no. 3, 521–42.

Snyder, J., F. Bolin, and K. Zumwalt. 1992. "Curriculum Implementation." In *Handbook of Research on Curriculum,* ed. P.W. Jackson, 402–35. Old Tappan, N.J.: Macmillan.

Thompson, S. 2001. "The Authentic Standards Movement and Its Evil Twin." *Phi Delta Kappan* 82, 358–62.

Chapter Three

The Impacts of Testing
on Teaching Practices

Last year, when I was a college student, I had great ideas using hands-on activities and cooperative learning in my classroom as a way to get students to be internally motivated for learning. With the testing programs we have in this school, there isn't much leeway for me to be creative or innovative and create excellent lessons. The test is the total goal. We spend time every day doing rote exercises. Forget ever doing hands-on activities, science or math games, or creative writing experiences. We do one hour of sit and drill in each of the subjects of math, reading, and writing. We use a basal reader, math workbook pages, and rote writing prompts. It is all step by step; the same thing every week. Every day for one hour the whole school does the exact same direct instruction lesson. No visitors are allowed in the classes. The children sit and get drilled over and over. I have to teach the letters by saying "A, what is A?" I repeat this over and over in a scripted lesson that my principal makes me use. I read exactly what they hear. You can't improvise, add, or take away. You do exactly what it says. This is how testing has impacted my school and my teaching. As a first year teacher I feel like I don't have a choice to deviate from this awful test preparation.

(Ann, a first-year teacher)

As the teacher in this quotation explained, testing has affected how she teaches. Research has also shown that testing can impact how teachers teach. For instance, as a result of the testing in North Carolina, 59 percent of elementary, middle, and high school teachers reported changing their teaching methods (Yarbrough, 1999). In another study of one North Carolina county, 74 percent of teachers reported changing their methods in writing, 52 percent in math, and 48 percent in reading (Jones and Johnston, 2002). Similarly, Barksdale-Ladd and Thomas (2000) found that 75 percent of teachers in two other large states changed their instructional practices in response to high-stakes testing. These changes in instructional practices suggest that many teachers are trying to adapt their teaching to meet the increasing demands of high-stakes testing. What is less clear, however, is whether these changes are having a positive or negative effect on teaching quality and student achievement. The purpose of this chapter is to investigate this issue to assess the impact of high-stakes testing on teaching methods, and subsequently, on students' learning.

EFFECTIVE TEACHING

Before one can accurately assess the effects of high-stakes testing on teaching practices, one must understand how students learn and which teaching methods are most effective in fostering student learning. Many current theories of teaching and learning embrace a student-centered, "constructivist" approach. Constructivists believe that students *actively construct* their knowledge through interacting with their physical and social environments (Piaget, 1973; Vygotsky, 1978), as opposed to being empty vessels into which knowledge is poured. Brooks and Brooks (1999) have identified many of the differences between constructivist classrooms and traditional classrooms and note that in constructivist classrooms, teachers present the curriculum from whole to part with an emphasis on the big concepts (as opposed to an emphasis on basic skills); listen to, value, and use student questions to drive the curriculum (as opposed to adhering to a rigid curriculum); allow students to use real-world raw data and manipulatives (as opposed to relying heavily on textbooks and workbooks); act as facilitators or guides who help mediate the learning environment for students (as opposed to acting as experts who dispense the "correct" information to students); assess students as they work and learn, as well as assessing them through portfolios of student work (as opposed to assessing only through tests at the end of the learning); and allow students to work in groups to learn from one another as well as the teacher (as opposed to having students work alone). Cognitive scientists (e.g., cognitive and developmental psychologists, computer scientists, neuroscientists) have also generated much research to confirm these basic principles of teaching and learning (see National Research Council, 2000 for further explanation).

Student-centered teaching approaches that are consistent with constructivist theories include cooperative learning (students working together in small groups to accomplish a goal); discussions; inquiry (students forming hypotheses and gathering data to solve a problem);

"hands-on" learning; and guided discovery (the teacher identifies a goal, arranges information so that patterns can be found, and guides students toward the goal) (Airasian and Walsh, 1997; Eggen and Kauchak, 2001).

In contrast to student-centered approaches, "teacher-centered" approaches place the teacher in a more central role during instruction. Teacher-centered methods of instruction include lecture; lecture-discussion (a combination of short lectures supplemented with teacher questioning); and direct instruction (used to teach skills that have a set of procedures that are developed through practice, such as adding fractions) (Eggen and Kauchak, 2001). These types of approaches are often advocated by testing proponents who want to get "back to the basics." As George W. Bush remarked: "The building blocks of knowledge were the same yesterday and will be the same tomorrow. We do not need trendy new theories or fancy experiments or feel-good curriculums. The basics work. If drill gets the job done, then rote is right" (cited in Coles, 2001, Bush and "The Basics" section, para. 2).

Which teaching methods are most effective? Both student-centered and teacher-centered approaches can be effective. Student-centered methods are more effective for complex goals that emphasize higher-order thinking and problem solving, and teacher-centered methods are more effective for teaching procedural skills and organized bodies of knowledge (topics that examine facts or concepts and the relationships among them) (Brophy and Good, 1986). Effective teachers use a balance of both of these methods, depending upon the goals and objectives of each lesson (Airasian and Walsh, 1997; Pressley, Rankin, and Yokoi, 1996). As Zemelman, Daniels, and Hyde (1998) summarized:

> To work toward the goal of "Best Practice," to embody the changes recommended in the curriculum reports we have cited, most teachers need to enrich their classroom repertoire in two directions (1) to set aside time and build classroom structures that support more *student-directed activity*; and (2) to make their *teacher-directed* activities both less predominant and more effective. We've seen that when teachers learn practical strategies to manage both of these modes of instruction, the curricular improvements they desire begin to take hold. (p. 212)

It is impossible to specify the precise balance of student-centered versus teacher-centered methods that are necessary for a "perfect" lesson. The balance will be different for each topic, subject, grade level, and group of students, depending upon the objectives of the lesson. However, recent research has shown the benefits of student-centered instruction (Wenglinsky, 2000), and most of the major professional teaching organizations and national standards (e.g., National Council of Teachers of Mathematics, 2000; National Research Council, 1996) have espoused philosophies consistent with constructivist theory and student-centered methods. Goldsmith (1999) has described the National Council of Teachers of Mathematics' (NCTM) 2000 standards by saying:

> Whereas traditional mathematics education focuses on memorization, rote learning, and the application of facts and procedures, the [NCTM] Standards-based approach emphasizes the development of conceptual understanding and reasoning. A corresponding pedagogical shift has moved the focus from direct instruction, drill, and practice toward more active student engagement with mathematical ideas through collaborative investigations, hands-on explorations, the use of multiple representations, and discussion and writing. . . . Nowhere do the Standards contend that computation is unimportant or that students can get by without knowing basic number facts and operations. They do, however, recommend diminishing the amount of class time dedicated to skills practice ("drill and kill") to make room for conceptual learning. (p. 40, 41)

In sum, while most educators recognize the need for both student-centered and teacher-centered methods, student-centered approaches are seen as an effective means to foster student learning and achievement, especially for higher-order thinking and problem solving.

In the sections that follow, we describe how teaching methods have changed in response to high-stakes testing—both negatively and positively.

NEGATIVE EFFECTS ON TEACHING

Teaching Methods

Some educators and researchers claim that the high-stakes testing environment has had a negative effect on students' achievement by causing teachers to focus on low-level knowledge and skills, resulting in less in-depth understanding and less focus on higher-order thinking skills. As one teacher in Texas reported, "TAAS [Texas Assessment of Academic Skills] is not higher-order thinking skills. It's less than what I would teach on a normal basis at that level" (Gordon and Reese, 1997). Critics of testing maintain that it forces teachers to focus predominantly on teacher-centered methods instead of student-centered practices; thus creating an imbalance in teaching methods. As a result, these educators argue that the unintended consequences of high-stakes tests are that they have hindered teachers' efforts to implement balanced teaching approaches. As Kohn (2000) wrote: "To be sure, many city schools that serve low-income children of color were second rate to begin with. Now, however, some of these schools in Chicago, Houston, Baltimore, and elsewhere, are arguably becoming third rate as the pressures of high-stakes testing lead to a more systematic use of low-level, drill-and-skill teaching, often in the context of packaged programs purchased by school districts" (p. 325).

A parent recently said that his third-grade daughter asked him: "Daddy, are we ever going to get to read books in the third grade or will we just be doing worksheets for the tests?" This question shows that even young students can be aware of testing and how it affects the instruction they receive. The following studies highlight specific examples of what some teachers and principals have said about this predominantly teacher-centered focus.

A teacher in one study noted that high-stakes tests are "giving bad teachers an excuse to continue doing what they've always done—lots of skill and drill. It's a license for bad teaching" (Barksdale-Ladd and Thomas, 2000, p. 389). A teacher in Texas reported similar outcomes of high-stakes testing: "We try to do hands-on kinds of things actively involving students, but we realize we have to spend lots of time on drill and practice with paper and pencil because of the way the test is formatted" (Gordon and Reese, 1997).

A principal in another study reported:

> The accountability system has an impact on everything we do. To focus on specific basic skills, you have to drill. We would like to get away from drill and pounding stuff into kids' heads; they don't remember it the next year. But if the accountability system looks at scores to judge school effectiveness, you can't take your eyes off of basic skills. (Mitchell, 1997, p. 263)

Other researchers have reported:

> Everywhere we turned, we heard stories of teachers who were being told, in the name of "raising standards," that they could no longer teach reading using the best of children's literature but instead must fill their classrooms and their days with worksheets, exercises, and drills. (Calkins, Montgomery, and Santman, 1998, pp. 2, 73)

Similar effects were reported by Wideen et al. (1997) based on classroom observations and interviews with teachers, principals, and students. They concluded: "high-stakes testing has led teachers away from strategies consistent with ['exemplary'] science teaching. We viewed 'exemplary' science teaching as that which uses an authentic approach to science, takes a constructivist view of how students learn science, and offers opportunities for active learning" (p. 440). They go on to state: "teachers reported not having time to use any strategy other than direct teaching" (p. 441).

Each of the previous examples illustrates that these teachers and principals are clearly frustrated by having to devote so much of their instruction to teacher-centered practices. In many cases, the reason for their frustration appears to be the negative effect that the teacher-centered methods are perceived to be having on the students. As one teacher commented:

> Learning for the tests isn't meaningful; it's a chore, and so I think the tests have really made achievement go down . . . the scores are up, but the kids [today] know less, and they are less as people . . . I think it's a crime; it's educational malpractice. (Barksdale-Ladd and Thomas, 2000, p. 392)

Similarly, another teacher commented: "I think we're hurting the kids, honestly. I mean our scores are better but I just don't think they have the well-rounded skills they'll need" (Perreault, 2000, p. 707).

In another school, located on a remote island, the sole science teacher for the small school explained to one of the authors of this book: "I used to do labs, but since testing, I don't do labs anymore. We don't have time." As a result, an island of students will go through schooling from grades kindergarten to twelve without experiencing inquiry-based laboratory science.

For some teachers, standardized tests seem incompatible with student-centered approaches to teaching. As an example, Passman (2001) described a case study of a fifth grade teacher who works with him to develop and implement a long-term inquiry project (a student-centered approach). The project was a complete success according to Passman, and the teacher remarked, "It's amazing how smart kids get when you teach 'em this way." Soon after the end of the project, the principal called a meeting in which he warned, "Don't teach anything that isn't on the Iowa test" (the high-stakes test for which the school was held accountable). Soon after this meeting, the teacher's classroom, which had been set up to facilitate student-centered approaches, was rearranged in rows and aisles as is typical in teacher-centered classrooms. When asked why she had changed the seating, the teacher remarked: "You were there when [the principal] told us to teach to the test. That's what I am doing, teaching to the test. This constructivist stuff is nice, but we have real work to do now!" Obviously this teacher saw student-centered approaches as being at odds with having students learn what was tested on the standardized test. As a result, she changed her teaching methods to reflect what was expected of her by her principal.

Teacher Creativity

Another negative unintended consequence of high-stakes tests is that the pressure felt by teachers has eroded their ability to teach creatively. Some teachers believe that if they do not teach with a certain method that their students will perform worse on the tests. Has high-stakes testing taken the art out of teaching? Some teachers claim that it has; for instance, one teacher reported:

> I'm not the teacher I used to be. I used to be great, and I couldn't wait to get to school every day because I loved being great at what I do. All of the most powerful teaching tools I used to use every day are no good to me now because they don't help children get ready for the test, and it makes me like a robot instead of a teacher. (Barksdale-Ladd and Thomas, 2000, p. 392)

This sentiment has been echoed by other teachers: "At my school, creativity is blown out the window" (Gordon and Reese, 1997). "It is very much a cookbook kind of approach—do this, do that, get those skills ingrained so kids will score better. It doesn't seem to have much to do with what kids need" (Perreault, 2000, p. 708). High school science teachers have reported that the testing reduced the opportunities for spontaneity and depth and "reduced the number of unusual and interesting things" that they were able to do (Wideen et al., 1997).

These cookbook strategies might also be having negative unintended consequences on students, who might be less likely to be creative themselves as a result of these teacher-centered methods. As one observer in an elementary school told one of the authors of this book: " 'How to get a good score' should be written across the entrance to the school. The skills the students are learning through the diagramming strategies are truly useful, but seem to impede imaginative learning. The children all want to share ideas, but they are forced to work in silence." This person recognized the need to teach the skill, but also acknowledged the limitations of teacher-centered approaches when students were confined to being taught by only this approach.

A fifth grade teacher in the Jones and Johnston (2002) study reported that her teaching methods had a negative impact on students' creativity and remarked that they "put down on paper only what they think they should, and not what they want . . . they're not learning to express their feelings and their emotions . . . they leave out the best parts of writing . . . they're learning to dread writing" (p. 8).

In sum, the negative effects of high-stakes testing on teaching practices can include an unbalanced emphasis on teacher-centered approaches and a reduction in teacher and student creativity.

POSITIVE EFFECTS ON TEACHING

In contrast to the studies cited above, some researchers have found testing to be instrumental in promoting *positive* changes in instructional methodologies. In fact, because of the testing, some teachers are changing their methods to more student-centered approaches. A survey of North Carolina teachers found that since the implementation of high-stakes testing, 26.8 percent of elementary teachers reported using more student-centered instruction, compared to only 12.1 percent who reported using less student-centered instruction (Jones et al., 1999). These results are contrary to those suggesting that testing is forcing teachers to use mainly teacher-centered approaches.

Firestone et al. (2001) studied fourth grade math and science teachers' instruction in New Jersey and found that "teaching to the test is encouraging teachers to consider more inquiry-oriented instructional practice" (p. 11). Specifically, teachers reported four general changes, all of which are more student-centered and consistent with constructivist theory: having students explain their thought processes; using manipulatives; problem solving; and working on students' writing. However, they cautioned that while teachers were exploring new student-centered options, traditional (more teacher-centered) instruction still predominated. Further, these student-centered strategies were often cosmetic in that teachers did not make deep changes in their practices (Schorr and Firestone, 2001). For instance, they often continued to assign the same kinds of math tasks that they had in the past, and their changes in classroom discourse often did not result in better-quality discourse.

Positive changes in teaching methods have also been reported in a study of two Kentucky teachers' math methods (Borko and Elliott, 1999). In response to Kentucky's curriculum standards and high-stakes testing program, one school's curriculum committee revised their mathematics curriculum, and as a result, one teacher claimed that they had "a much tighter, more comprehensive math program" (Borko and Elliott,

1999, p. 396). Moreover, the changes in the school's math program were accompanied by "substantial changes" in teachers' teaching methods. As one of the teachers described:

> We had to devote a lot of time to talking about math and talking about solving problems and solving problems in different ways. I'd say our computation instruction is maybe 20 percent to 30 percent of what we do, whereas before it was expected to be about 80 percent of what we did. So that's flipped completely. (p. 396)

These changes are consistent with NCTM's 2000 standards, which recommend reducing time spent on skills practice (computation instruction) to make room for conceptual learning. As a result of these methods changes, these two teachers believed that their students had a better understanding of math. The scores of their school's students on the high-stakes test verified their beliefs; their math scores increased ten points in one year. As one teacher said, "We felt it just validated what we had done with our math curriculum" (Borko and Elliott, 1999, p. 396).

Another study of Kentucky teachers examined writing instruction and found that since the implementation of the statewide assessments that require writing portfolios, "students were spending more time on higher-level writing activities involving the composition of extended text and less time on lower-level activities such as filling in workbooks and worksheets and copying from the board" (Bridge, Compton-Hall, and Cantrell, 1997, p. 151).

In one North Carolina county, teachers were asked about the specific effects that the high-stakes testing program had on their instruction in each subject area (Jones and Johnston, 2002). Teachers made the most methods changes in writing (74 percent of teachers), followed by math (52 percent of teachers), reading (48 percent of teachers), science (26 percent of teachers), and social studies (17 percent of teachers). Some teachers tried more student-centered approaches, while others tried more teacher-centered approaches. For instance, of the teachers who made changes to their instructional methods in reading, 11 percent said that they had become more skill-driven (more teacher-centered), while another 11 percent said that they focused more on discussion as a means of teaching reading comprehension (more student-centered).

The percentage of teachers who reported that students learned more as a result of the methods changes was 100 percent for math, 87 percent for writing, 70 percent for reading, 50 percent for science, and 25 percent for social studies (Jones and Johnston, 2002). One teacher explained:

I don't really think that in second grade I taught writing very well. I never taught the skill of how to sit down and compose a good paragraph. I actually feel like I'm teaching writing a lot more now than just looking at their journals and saying developmentally this is where they are [as I did in the past]. (p. 6)

Furthermore, Jones and Johnston (2002) found that the majority of teachers who made changes in their teaching methods due to high-stakes testing reported that the overall quality of their teaching had improved in the subjects that were tested (reading, writing, and math). In fact, in mathematics, all of the teachers who had changed their methods believed that the changes had improved the quality of their teaching of mathematics. The results were less positive for the subjects not tested (i.e., science and social studies), often because teachers reported spending less time on these subjects and more time on the subjects tested.

To summarize, some teachers have reported that they have made positive methodological changes in response to high-stakes testing. In some cases, teachers have implemented more student-centered methods and practices that are consistent with standards such as NCTM 2000. Other teachers are trying more teacher-centered approaches and believe that these methods are appropriate and have improved the quality of their instruction. Either way, testing has influenced some teachers to make methodological changes that they believe to be beneficial to their students.

LITTLE TO NO EFFECTS ON TEACHING

In the previous two sections, we discussed how testing can affect teachers' teaching practices in a negative and a positive manner. These studies indicate that testing can affect teaching practices. Other researchers, however, have found testing to have little to no effect on teachers' teaching methodologies (e.g., Firestone, Mayrowetz, and Fairman, 1998; Grant, 2001). As noted previously, Jones and Johnston (2002) found that 74 percent of teachers changed their teaching methods in writing. Of course this implies that 26 percent of teachers did *not* change their teaching methods in writing. Similarly, only about half of the teachers in this study changed their methods in reading and mathematics in response to the high-stakes testing. A teacher in another study explained her response to the testing in the following manner:

I pretty much just teach what I teach. I'm pretty dramatic and creative and I have decided as I've experienced these changes the last few years that I just cannot let the [high-stakes tests] dominate the way I teach. So I just refuse to let it squeeze all creative subjects out of my classroom and so we still do them. (Yarbrough, 1999, p. 70)

These types of studies remind us that while many teachers appear to be changing their teaching practices, the full extent of these changes is unclear. As discussed previously, some teachers appear to be making cosmetic changes, not deep changes in their practices (Schorr and Firestone, 2001). Further research is needed to help clarify under what conditions testing has the most and least effects on teaching practices. The next section discusses some of the major factors that appear to affect teaching practices within the context of high-stakes testing.

FACTORS INFLUENCING CHANGES IN TEACHING

So far, the evidence presented in this chapter has indicated that testing has had a negative effect on some teaching practices, a positive effect on others, and not much of an effect on still others. In this section, we take a closer look at the research to identify some of the factors that might influence how testing affects teaching practices.

Limitations

Before we investigate the factors influencing changes in teaching, it is important to recognize the difficulties in trying to make a definitive assessment of the impact of testing on teaching methods. First, there has been relatively little research on how high-stakes testing has affected teachers' instructional methods. Clearly, more research needs to be conducted in this area. In addition, much of the research presented in this chapter relies on the self-reports (i.e., interviews and surveys) of teachers and principals who might not be as objective as an independent observer.

Secondly, each state has developed its own standards and has used different types of tests to assess students on these standards (see *Education Week* Editors, 2001). Moreover, states assess students at different grade levels and have different levels of accountability in different subject areas (some states do not test in science or social studies). Consequently, the types and content of questions vary, along with the pressure associated with the test. All of these factors contribute differently to affecting teachers' methods of instruction.

Finally, other factors influence teachers' teaching practices besides high-stakes tests, and these factors can confound the results of the research in this area. For instance, teachers' approaches to teaching can vary according to the grade level at which they teach; their knowledge, beliefs, experience, status, and position as teachers; and the expectations of the district, school, and community (see Cimbricz, 2002 for further explanation).

With these caveats in mind, we identified four factors that appear to influence the type and amount of changes teachers make to their teaching methodologies: 1) the type of high-stakes assessment; 2) the type of professional development teachers receive; 3) the subject area tested; and 4) the level of achievement of the school.

Types of High-Stakes Assessment

There is reason to believe that the *type* of high-stakes test might affect teachers' instructional practices. Portfolios, essays, and tests that allow students to show their work with open-ended questions generally influence methods changes in a more positive, student-centered direction than multiple-choice questions that focus on low-level facts and skills.

In the earlier section entitled "Negative Effects on Teaching," we presented evidence of how some teachers and principals believe that tests focusing on low-level facts and skills negatively influence changes in teachers' teaching methods. In this section, we present examples of how other forms of assessment have been shown to foster positive changes in teachers' methods.

Portfolios. Portfolio assessments are a collection of works from a student and often include a student's classroom work, revisions, assessments, and reflections on his or her learning.

Teachers in one Kentucky study described how they used the state's math portfolios (used as part of the state's testing program during the 1995–1996 school year) to make changes to their instructional methods (Borko and Elliott, 1999). The portfolio included "a table of contents; a letter to the reviewer written by the student to describe the portfolio; and five to seven entries showing breadth in core content areas, types of tasks (e.g., investigations, applications, nonroutine problems), and tools (e.g., calculators, models, manipulatives, measurement instruments)" (p. 395). The two teachers in this study treated the portfolios "as an integral part of their mathematics program" (p. 396). Although the teachers faced struggles in implementing the portfolios, both teachers were upset that the portfolios were discontinued as part of the high-stakes assessment in Kentucky. As one teacher remarked:

> Now they've come out and said they don't want math portfolios as part of the assessment. I'm really uncomfortable with that, because teachers aren't going to keep portfolios in their mathematics programs. There's no accountability. If there's no accountability, it's not going to happen. (Borko and Elliott, 1999, p. 400)

These teachers believed not only that the portfolios positively impacted their teaching methods, but also that the portfolio assessments were essential to holding teachers accountable.

Bridge, Compton-Hall, and Cantrell (1997) attributed several positive outcomes to the changes teachers made in their writing instruction due to the Kentucky Education Reform Act (KERA) of 1990, which required writing portfolios as well as written short-answer responses to open-ended questions in all of the tested subjects. They found that students spent twice as much time writing and that teachers spent twice as much time teaching writing. Further, students spent more time on higher-level writing activities and conferring with teachers and peers about revising and editing their work. Bridge and her colleagues suggested that the changes in the assessment practices in Kentucky and Vermont (which also used portfolio assessment) were positive and that they "may serve as a catalyst for teachers to move toward a process approach to the teaching of writing" (p. 168). They go on to state that "In the past teachers often felt restricted by standardized assessments of writing that focused on isolated skills, such as selecting correct grammar or punctuation for a provided piece of writing" (p. 168). In contrast, portfolio assessments for writing are more consistent with effective teaching methods. As Bridge, Compton-Hall, and Cantrell explain, "Portfolio assessments more nearly match what is known about the development of writing; they enable both teachers and students to evaluate the progress students have made over time and their ability to bring a given piece from first draft to final form" (p. 168).

Why don't more states use portfolios as part of their high-stakes assessment? Although there are many advantages to using portfolio assessments, they are difficult to use as a large-scale assessment for a few major reasons. First, portfolios are more expensive to "grade" than typical multiple-choice tests because each portfolio must be scored by a rater (and usually two raters are used). In contrast, multiple-choice tests can be graded by a machine. Second, obtaining reliable scores on portfolios has proved difficult. Reliability refers to the consistency of measurement of the scores and is important if one is to trust that the measurement of student learning is accurate. If scores for an individual are variable, it is important to know whether or not the variability is due to the test design or actual changes in an individual's learning. Portfolios and other types of authentic assessments have greater subjectivity in the scoring process (than a machine-graded multiple-choice item) and, as a result, tend to have a lower reliability than a multiple-choice test that has items that are clearly correct or incorrect.

An evaluation of the 1992 Vermont Portfolio Assessment program found that the reliability coefficients (which ranged from 0.33 to 0.43) were disappointingly low (Koretz et al., 1993). These findings led Koretz et al. to conclude: "Rater reliability is low enough to undermine the utility of 1992 scores for comparing groups of students (schools, districts, or other groups)" (p. 18). Unfortunately, these two factors, cost and reliability, remain large hurdles to making the use of portfolios a reality in many states. These factors do not, however, preclude teachers from using portfolios as part of their normal instruction and assessment.

Essays and Writing Rubrics. One elementary teacher in Washington used sample writing test prompts to guide her writing instruction (Borko and Stecher, 2001, p. 7). After students responded to the sample prompt, they scored their essays with the teacher, using the same scoring rubric the state used to score the essays at the end of the year. Students worked in groups to discuss which strategies were successful, and the teacher made the connection from the state scoring to the students' writing. Another teacher who also used the state's scoring rubric as part of her instruction explained how she talked to the students about what they could do to raise their scores and used higher-scoring essays as examples. In fact, more than 50 percent of the teachers in this study used rubric-based approaches to teach writing. According to the teachers, the results had been good: "The students are really making some positive changes. You can just see how motivated they are, and how they're so much more able to communicate" (Borko and Stecher, 2001, p. 7). Although the study did not evaluate Washington state's writing scoring rubrics, the teachers in this study appeared to be satisfied with using it as part of their writing instruction. The study did not present results as to how students scored on the high-stakes writing tests.

Similarly, the Pennsylvania System of School Assessment (PSSA) encourages teachers to use the statewide writing assessment to inform their teaching and to serve as a model for assessment development. For the writing assessment, students must write an essay in response to prompts or open-ended writing assignments. The essays are scored by two raters using a rubric. Interestingly, teachers who were trained about the process of how the essays were scored using the rubric more strongly agreed than nontrained teachers that the state writing assessment had influenced them and had improved their ability to teach writing (Lumley and Yan, 2001). Furthermore, they agreed more strongly than nontrained teachers that the writing assessment had improved the writing ability and skills of their students. Lumley and Yan (2001) also noted, however: "even though many teachers agree with the beliefs and values of holistic scoring and the characteristics of effective writing, they are reluctant to *fully* use the state [writing] rubric, descriptors and writing samples as the basis for classroom instruction of those skills and characteristics" (p. 18, emphasis added). They speculated that this reluctance to fully use the state's materials might be due to the facts that: 1) there are weaknesses in the materials provided by the state, 2) teachers are using their own materials (rubrics and samples), or 3) teachers are clinging to their traditional methods and not fully adopting a holistic approach to writing instruction.

While some teachers have used state rubrics as the basis for their classroom instruction, others have not integrated them as seamlessly, and instead provided test preparation activities separate from their regular instruction (Koretz, Mitchell, Barron, and Keith, 1996; Torrance, 1993). Therefore, it appears unrealistic to expect all teachers to use the same methods and strategies to teach in the same manner. One way of influencing classroom practices is to provide ongoing and intensive training to help teachers make the connection between quality assessments and effective teaching practices (Fuchs, Fuchs, Karns, Hamlett, and Katzaroff, 1999; Lumley and Yan, 2001). We discuss this type of training in the "Professional Development" section below.

Cautions about Writing Rubrics. Not all writing rubrics are equally effective in promoting quality writing instruction. As one teacher explained, "Sometimes I get the impression the rubrics were written by people who haven't been in a high school English classroom since Moses was a baby. They don't know what quality is in a student paper" (Mabry, 1999, p. 677). Comments such as these remind us of the importance of rubrics that promote quality writing instruction.

Mabry (1999) further questions the use of writing rubrics as a valid measure of students' writing:

> Rubrics standardize scoring, and so they standardize writing. But standardized writing, by definition, is not good writing because good writing features individual expression, which is not standardized. The standardization of any skill

that is fundamentally individual obstructs its assessment. And this presents a validity problem because the assessment fails to produce scores that support valid inferences about students' writing achievement. More specifically, it is a problem of construct validity—testing not the construct of *writing achievement* but the construct of *compliance to the rubric*. (p. 678)

Science Investigations. High-stakes tests are often criticized because in some cases they emphasize the teaching of basic facts and knowledge that is considered "low-level" (as compared to higher-order thinking skills and problem solving). The Michigan Educational Assessment Program (MEAP) had addressed this problem in an interesting manner in their fifth grade science test. During the school year, all fifth grade students completed the same science investigation. As an example, to conduct an investigation entitled "Reducing Friction Investigation," teachers were provided with a teacher's guide, a student journal for each student, and the materials necessary to conduct the investigation. The student journal listed the materials, described the procedure, and asked students questions regarding the investigation. The teacher's guide provided instructions on how to conduct the investigation, along with sample answers to the questions in the student journal. After the students completed the investigation and their journals, they handed in the journals to their teacher. These student journals were then handed back to the students on the day of the MEAP science test so that they could use them to answer questions specifically addressing that investigation. The MEAP science test consisted of many questions, only a few of which pertained to the investigation. Unfortunately, a January 2002 report of MEAP stated: "MEAP science no longer has the budget to include a hands-on science investigation for students in Grades 5 and 8 to conduct prior to taking their MEAP science test" (MEAP, 2002, p. 4). Nonetheless, providing students with the opportunity for real-world investigations is an interesting idea that could be developed further in other assessment situations.

Summary of Alternative Assessments. These cases illustrate that high-stakes testing *can* have a positive impact on teachers' instructional methods. However, as was noted in the "Negative Effects on Teaching" section, not all tests have this positive impact. This section on alternative assessments was not intended to be a comprehensive review of alternative assessments. Rather, it was included to show some of the possibilities that exist. The goal of state education departments and test developers should be to create tests that foster positive changes in teachers' approaches to instruction and that are in line with professional education standards. Both the portfolio and writing rubric appear to be possible solutions towards this goal. This suggestion is consistent with Schorr and Firestone's (2001) conclusion:

> If state testing is to continue as part of the landscape, and there is considerable evidence to suggest that it will continue spreading if anything, then such tests should include short open-ended or (even better) more challenging perform-ance-based items. Such items at least sensitize teachers to the need to consider strategies that differ from conventional practice even if they do not help teach-ers develop the level of understanding to embed such strategies in a substan-tially revised instructional approach. (p. 22)

These recommendations for tests to become assessments of students' thought processes and authentic work (e.g., portfolios) are consistent with constructivist learning theories and student-centered approaches. From a constructivist's perspective, it is difficult to measure one's knowl-edge with a one-time, multiple-choice exam. As Airasian and Walsh (1997) explained, "To convey one's construction of meaning will require an in-depth presentation about one's knowledge and how one arrived at or justifies that knowledge. If constructions are reduced to multiple-choice items or to some other truncated representational form, the rich-ness and meaning of constructivism will be lost" (p. 448).

Type of Professional Development

Taken as a whole, the results presented in this chapter suggest that teach-ers will change their methods in response to the testing. However, as we discussed previously, some teachers' changes are mainly cosmetic and affect content more than they effect deep changes in their practices. Schorr and Firestone (2001) found that often an important link in pro-moting positive change was lacking: professional development. For instance, teachers in Maine and Maryland found weaknesses in the pro-fessional development that they received (Firestone and Mayrowetz, 2000). This has led Schorr and Firestone (2001) to recommend that (in the context of their study of math teachers) "it is important to provide the kind of intensive professional development focusing on mathemati-cal content, children's learning of that content, and strategies for helping children that has been shown to enhance student learning" (p. 22).

Bridge, Compton-Hall, and Cantrell (1997) concluded that it was unlikely that teachers in their study could have made the positive changes that they did in response to the new statewide writing assess-ment (including portfolios and written short essays in response to open-ended questions) without the increased money the state provided for staff development. "Teachers who did not already have the requisite knowledge about writing instruction indicated that they would not have been able to make instructional changes regardless of the mandates if they had not been provided with supportive staff development" (p. 169).

Interestingly, voluntary professional development activities (i.e., mentoring younger teachers, attending workshops and district-provided professional development that focuses specifically on content and instructional strategies in math or science) encouraged inquiry-oriented (student-centered) teaching in fourth grade math and science and discouraged direct math teaching (Firestone, Monfils, and Camilli, 2001). These results are encouraging and suggest that professional development is a viable means of effecting positive changes in teaching methodologies. Other researchers have also found professional development to be an important characteristic of successful schools (Kelley et al., 2000).

Firestone, Monfils, and Camilli (2001) cautioned, however, that not all professional development is the same. They found that professional development that focused specifically on preparing students for the state testing supported student-centered approaches as well as more teacher-centered approaches. "Insofar as the state test requires more showing of work and writing to provide explanations of mathematical and scientific reasoning as well as justifications for solution methods, these sessions appear to support more inquiry-oriented instruction, but the significant portion of the test devoted to more recall-oriented multiple-choice items also supports more direct instruction" (Firestone, Monfils, and Camilli, 2001, p. 28). Accordingly, professional development can encourage positive changes in methods but does not ensure it if the focus is to teach low-level knowledge.

If professional development is to be effective in promoting lasting change, it must be sustained and supported over long periods of time. Reform by testing rarely allows the kind of time needed to sustain meaningful change in education. The implication is that politicians who demand accountability and improvement must also provide money and resources to support teachers' professional development.

Subject Area

Studies that noted positive effects on teaching methods often included or focused on mathematics. For instance, two studies we cited previously (Borko and Elliott, 1999; Firestone et al., 2001) as studies that found some positive effects specifically reported about teachers' mathematics instruction. Moreover, while Jones and Johnston (2002) interviewed elementary teachers about all subjects that they taught (reading, writing, math, science, and social studies), they found that *all* of the teachers who changed their instructional techniques in mathematics believed that their students were learning more as a result. In none of the other subjects did all of the teachers make this claim.

It is also necessary to examine the subject areas of the teachers who reported more negative effects of the testing on their instructional practice. Looking back at the studies we cited previously in the "Negative Effects on Teaching" section, all of the elementary and middle-grades teachers in the Barksdale-Ladd and Thomas (2000) study taught reading, writing, and language arts—*not* mathematics. Wideen et al. (1997) studied eighth, tenth, and twelfth grade *science* teachers, and Passman (2001) studied a teacher working on an inquiry project on explorers, which appeared to focus more on reading, writing, and social studies and much less on math.

Although it is difficult to draw any definitive conclusions based on this limited number of studies, there appears to be a trend that teachers reported making more positive changes in their mathematics instruction than in other subjects. One explanation for this finding could be the emphasis on skills in mathematics and the relative ease with which mathematics can be tested in objective, large-scale assessments. In contrast, knowledge and skills in other subjects such as writing tend to be more difficult to assess on a large-scale objective test.

Level of School Achievement

Another theme that emerged from the studies of teachers' instructional methods was that teachers at lower-performing and/or higher-poverty schools were making more changes to their teaching practices than teachers at higher-performing schools. Very few studies have examined this difference explicitly; therefore, the results presented in this section may not be generalizable to all situations.

In a study of elementary, middle, and high school teachers, 908 teachers who had taught prior to the introduction of high-stakes testing in their state responded to questions about how they had changed their teaching practices since the implementation of high-stakes testing (Yarbrough, 1999). Teachers at lower-performing schools reported making more changes than teachers in higher-performing schools and generally reported changing to more student-centered types of instruction.

In contrast, Perreault (2000) found that at the low-performing schools, principals encouraged teacher-centered approaches that focused on skills. However, principals at higher-scoring schools "tended to reinforce teacher attempts at enrichment and relief from the focus on testing, but only if scores remained high" (p. 708). Thus, although teachers at both types of these schools felt the pressure of testing, principals were less likely to interfere in teachers' instruction if the results were successful.

In another study, teachers at lower-ranked schools reported changing to student-centered approaches *and* teacher-centered approaches (Jones and Johnston, 2002). In addition, they generally found these changes to be effective in improving instruction.

Higher-Poverty Schools. There is also increasing evidence that test preparation practices are more often used where more than 60 percent of the students are members of minorities (Rothman, 1996; Soloman, 1998; Firestone et al., 2001). Other researchers report that high-poverty schools with the lowest scores are often victims of more test preparation (International Reading Association, 1999). A study by Firestone et al. (2001) found a substantial association between teaching to the test and poor school districts. Furthermore, the Firestone study showed that these poorest schools tended to use more teacher-centered approaches.

Schools in poor communities typically have less financial support for education and serve children who enter school without the types of experiences that lead to success in school. When these schools are placed under the chopping block of high-stakes assessment, these children are then further disadvantaged by frequent test preparation practices. Kohn (2000) maintains that schools that serve low-income children of color are "becoming third rate as testing pressures lead to a more systematic use of low-level, drill-and-skill teaching, often in the context of packaged programs purchased by school districts . . . Thus when someone emphasizes the importance of 'higher expectations' for minority children, we might reply, 'Higher expectations to do what? Bubble-in more ovals correctly on a bad test—or pursue engaging projects that promote sophisticated thinking?' " (p. 47).

Ann (whose quotation appears at the beginning of this chapter) is a new teacher at a North Carolina city school that serves children in poverty. Ann said she believed that if they would just let her, she could teach her children the reading, writing, and mathematics skills they needed. She felt as if her teacher education program had given her a variety of skills for teaching the low-income children her school served, but the rigid implementation of test preparation materials prohibited her from doing what she believed was best. Although this type of rigid test preparation may provide better instruction than some children received before the implementation of high-stakes testing, many teachers like Ann find that administrative mandates for test preparation keep them from providing the quality of instruction that they would otherwise choose for their students.

While the data are limited, there appears to be a trend that there are more changes in instruction at the lower-performing and/or higher-poverty schools than at the higher-performing schools. One explanation for this trend is that the stakes are often higher at these schools, with principals, teachers, and students working under intense public scrutiny to raise achievement scores.

CONCLUSION

It is impossible to make sweeping generalizations about how high-stakes testing has affected teaching methodologies. Some studies have shown that testing leads teachers to make negative changes in their teaching practices, while other studies indicate that it leads teachers to make more positive ones, or few changes at all. As outlined in this chapter, some of the major factors that appear to affect how teachers change their teaching practices include: 1) the type of high-stakes assessment; 2) the type of professional development teachers receive; 3) the subject area being tested; and 4) the level of achievement of the school.

Hopefully, test developers will continue to improve upon test designs and create tests that encourage positive changes in teaching methodologies consistent with current learning theories. In addition, educational leaders should advocate for the time, money, and resources needed to help teachers make *meaningful* changes in instructional methodologies.

REFERENCES

Airasian, P., and M. Walsh. 1997. "Constructivist Cautions." *Phi Delta Kappan* 78, no. 6, 444–49.

Barksdale-Ladd, M. A., and K. F. Thomas. 2000. "What's at Stake in High-Stakes Testing: Teachers and Parents Speak Out." *Journal of Teacher Education* 51, 384–97.

Borko, H., and R. Elliott. 1999. "Hands-On Pedagogy versus Hands-Off Accountability: Tensions between Competing Commitments for Exemplary Math Teachers in Kentucky." *Phi Delta Kappan* 80, 394–400.

Borko, H., and B. Stecher. 2001. "Looking at Reform through Different Methodological Lenses: Surveys and Case Studies of the Washington State Education Reform." Paper presented at the meeting of the American Educational Research Association, Seattle, Wash., April.

Bridge, C. A., M. Compton-Hall, and S. C. Cantrell. 1997. "Classroom Writing Practices Revisited: The Effects of Statewide Reform on Writing Instruction." *The Elementary School Journal* 98, no. 2, 151–70.

Brooks, J. G., and M. G. Brooks. 1999. *In Search of Understanding: The Case for Constructivist Classrooms*. Upper Saddle River, N.J.: Merrill Prentice Hall.

Brophy, J., and T. L. Good. 1986. "Teacher Behavior and Student Achievement." In *Handbook of Research on Teaching* (3rd ed.), ed. M. Wittrock, 328–75. New York: Macmillan.

Calkins, L., K. Montgomery, and D. Santman. 1998. *A Teacher's Guide to Standardized Reading Tests: Knowledge Is Power*. Portsmouth, N.H.: Heinemann.

Cimbricz, S. 2002. "State-Mandated Testing and Teachers' Beliefs and Practice." *Education Policy Analysis Archives* 10, no. 2 (9 January). epaa.asu.edu/epaa/v10n2.html (accessed 11 April 2002).

Coles, G. 2001. "Learning to Read—'Scientifically.'" *Rethinking Schools* 15, no. 4 (Summer). www.rethinkingschools.org/Archives/15_04/Read154.htm (accessed 3 August 2002).

Education Week Editors. 2001. "Gaining Ground." *Education Week* 20, no. 17 (January): 33–40.

Eggen, P., and D. Kauchak. 2001. *Educational Psychology: Windows on Classrooms*. Upper Saddle River, N.J.: Merrill Prentice Hall.

Firestone, W. A., and D. Mayrowetz. 2000. "Rethinking 'High Stakes': Lessons from the United States and England and Wales." *Teachers College Record* 102, no. 4, 724–49.

Firestone, W., D. Mayrowetz, and J. Fairman. 1998. "Performance-Based Assessment and Instructional Change: The Effects of Testing in Maine and Maryland." *Educational Evaluation and Policy Analysis* 20, no. 2, 95–113.

Firestone, W. A., L. Monfils, and G. Camilli. 2001. "Pressure, Support, and Instructional Change in the Context of a State Testing Program." Paper presented at the meeting of the American Educational Research Association, Seattle, Wash., April.

Firestone, W. A., L. Monfils, G. Camilli, R. Schorr, J. Hicks, and D. Mayrowetz. 2001. "The Ambiguity of Test Preparation: A Multimethod Analysis in One State." Paper presented at the meeting of the American Educational Research Association, Seattle, Wash., April.

Fuchs, L. S., D. Fuchs, K. Karns, C. L. Hamlett, and M. Katzaroff. 1999. "Mathematics Performance Assessment in the Classroom: Effects on Teacher Planning and Student Problem Solving." *American Educational Research Journal* 36, 609–46.

Goldsmith, L. T. 1999. "What Is a Standards-Based Mathematics Curriculum?" *Educational Leadership* 57, no. 3, 40–44.

Gordon, S. P., and M. Reese. 1997. "High-Stakes Testing: Worth the Price?" *Journal of School Leadership* 7, 345–68.

Grant, S. G. 2001. "An Uncertain Lever: Exploring the Influence of State-Level Testing on Teaching Social Studies." *Teachers College Record* 103, no. 3, 398–426.

International Reading Association. 1999. "High-Stakes Assessments in Reading: A Position Statement." *Reading Teacher* 53, no. 3, 257–64.

Jones, B. D., and A. F. Johnston. 2002. "The Effects of High-Stakes Testing on Instructional Practices." Paper presented at the 2002 annual meeting of the American Educational Research Association, New Orleans, April.

Jones, G. M., B. D. Jones, B. H. Hardin, L. Chapman, T. Yarbrough, and M. Davis. 1999. "The Impact of High-Stakes Testing on Teachers and Students in North Carolina." *Phi Delta Kappan* 81, 199–203.

Kelley, C., A. Odden, A. Milanowski, and H. Heneman. 2000. "The Motivational Effects of School-Based Performance Awards." *Policy Briefs,* Graduate School of Education, University of Pennsylvania, Consortium for Policy Research in Education.

Kohn, A. 2000. "Standardized Testing and Its Victims." *Education Week* 20, no. 4 (27 September), 46–47, 60.

Koretz, D., D. McCaffrey, S. Klein, R. Bell, and B. Stecher. 1993. *The Reliability of Scores from the 1992 Vermont Portfolio Assessment Program* (CSE Technical Report 355). Los Angeles, Calif.: National Center for Research on Evaluation, Standards, and Student Testing (CRESST), University of California.

Koretz, D., K. Mitchell, S. Barron, and S. Keith. 1996. *Final Report: Perceived Effects of the Maryland School Performance Assessment Program.* Los Angeles, Calif.: National Center for Research on Evaluation, Standards, and Student Testing (CRESST), University of California.

Lumley, D. R., and W. Yan. 2001. "The Impact of State Mandated, Large-Scale Writing Assessment Policies in Pennsylvania." Paper presented at the meeting of the American Educational Research Association, Seattle, Wash., April.

Mabry, L. 1999. "Writing to the Rubric: Lingering Effects of Traditional Standardized Testing on Direct Writing Assessment." *Phi Delta Kappan* 80, 673–79.

Michigan Educational Assessment Program. 2002. *MEAP Update* 14, no. 2 (January). www.meritaward.state.mi.us/mma/meapinfo/update/0201-update.pdf (accessed 3 August 2002).

Mitchell, K. J. 1997. "What Happens When School Reform and Accountability Testing Meet?" *Theory into Practice* 36, no. 4, 262–65.

National Council of Teachers of Mathematics. 2000. *Principles and Standards in School Mathematics.* Reston, Va: National Council of Teachers of Mathematics.

National Research Council. 1996. *National Science Education Standards.* Washington, D.C.: National Academy Press.

National Research Council. 2000. *How People Learn.* Washington, D.C.: National Academy Press.

Passman, R. 2001. "Experiences with Student-Centered Teaching and Learning in High-Stakes Assessment Environments." *Education* 122, no. 1, 189–211.

Perreault, G. 2000. "The Classroom Impact of High-Stakes Testing." *Education* 120, no. 4, 705–10.

Piaget, J. 1973. *To Understand Is to Invent.* New York: Grossman.

Pressley, M., J. Rankin, and L. Yokoi. 1996. "A Survey of Instructional Practice of Primary Teachers Nominated as Effective in Promoting Literacy." *Elementary School Journal* 96, no. 4, 363–84.

Rothman, R. 1996. "Taking Aim at Testing." *American School Board Journal* 183, no. 2, 27–30.

Schorr, R. Y., and W. A. Firestone. 2001. "Changing Mathematics Teaching in Response to a State Testing Program: A Fine-Grained Analysis." Paper presented at the meeting of the American Educational Research Association, Seattle, Wash., April.

Soloman, P. 1998. *The Curriculum Bridge: From Standards to Actual Classroom Practice.* Thousand Oaks, Calif.: Corwin.

Torrance, H. 1993. "Combining Measurement-Driven Instruction with Authentic Assessment: Some Initial Observations of National Assessment in England and Wales." *Educational Evaluation and Policy Analysis* 15, 81–90.

Vygotsky, L. 1978. *Mind in Society: The Development of Higher Psychological Processes.* Cambridge, Mass.: Harvard University Press.

Wenglinsky, H. 2000. *How Teaching Matters: Bringing the Classroom Back into Discussions of Teacher Quality.* Princeton, N.J.: Educational Testing Service.

Wideen, M. F., T. O'Shea, I. Pye, and G. Ivany. 1997. "High-Stakes Testing and the Teaching of Science." *Canadian Journal of Education* 22, no. 4, 428–44.

Yarbrough, T. L. 1999. "Teacher Perceptions of the North Carolina ABC Program and the Relationship to Classroom Practice." Ph.D. dissertation, University of North Carolina at Chapel Hill.

Zemelman, S., H. Daniels, and A. Hyde. 1998. *Best Practice: New Standards for Teaching and Learning in America's Schools.* Portsmouth, N.H.: Heinemann.

Chapter Four

Truth or Consequences: Preparing for the Tests

> One thing I have noticed in our school is that testing is the ultimate goal for our kids. It seems like even first and second grade teachers are held accountable for where the fifth graders will be. What we are doing now is teaching children strategies to help them with end-of-grade tests. We use the strategies so that they can do better. Not that they write creatively or use different techniques to write, but we teach them the formula they will need to use on the test.
>
> (Anna, a North Carolina first grade teacher)

Teachers are often pressured and sometimes required by principals, district officials, and state administrators to dedicate significant amounts of time preparing students for high-stakes tests. On a surface level, the procedure of preparing students for the tests might appear innocuous. After all, it seems only fair for teachers to prepare students with the knowledge and skills measured on high-stakes tests. However, the reality of test preparation is much more complex than this. The purpose of this chapter is to unravel some of these complexities by providing a discussion of three of the major unintended consequences related to test preparation. First, we provide examples and explanations of how test preparation has taken time away from content instruction. Second, we discuss how practicing specifically for a test can invalidate the interpretation of the test scores. Third, we discuss some of the ethical issues related to test preparation. We conclude with a discussion of how much test preparation is appropriate.

TIME USED TO PREPARE FOR TESTS

Three weeks prior to the administration of the North Carolina end-of-grade tests, teachers at a North Carolina middle school held a series of pep rallies for the tests. The stakes were high for this school. If students did not score high enough to meet the state's standards, then the state could take over the school, replace the principal, prevent students from moving to the next grade level, require students to attend mandatory summer school, and/or keep teachers from receiving salary bonuses. In addition, the scores were published in the local newspapers, and the school's reputation in the community was at stake. Year after year this particular school had very high scores on tests, and although these students would likely do well on the tests regardless of test preparation, the teachers engaged in significant test preparation activities anyway. On one particular Monday, the sixth grade teachers dressed up as characters from the television show *Mission: Impossible* with black briefcases and black sunglasses and danced their way into a room filled with students to the *Mission: Impossible* theme music. The purpose of the all-day rally, according to the teachers, was to make sure that students took the test seriously and that students had one last chance to sharpen their test-taking skills.

This school's test preparation started at the beginning of the year at the parent-teacher open house, where parents were provided with information about the tests and how students should prepare for the tests. The State Department of Public Instruction provided each school with leaflets of information that were sent home to parents after the open house. The local school system then sent out a letter to parents with testing dates and information. This was followed by school newsletters that were sent home throughout the year filled with testing information. Students were taught the specific skills that would be tested, and each child went through three full practice test simulations before the final test. In place of the school's usual student advisory program, seven teachers provided instruction on aspects of the testing program, including information on guessing, how tests are scored, memorizing formulas, using highlighters, and regulating their time during the test. For students who were identified as needing extra preparation, an Individualized Educational Plan was developed to outline specific strategies for the student. The plan was then signed by parents and teachers and was implemented. For those students who were at the most risk of failure on the test, the plan included pulling them out of science or social studies for half of the year to work with a special tutor on mathematics and language arts.

As the testing day approached, students were repeatedly told to get a good night's rest, to wear comfortable clothing, and to plan to eat breakfast. No homework was assigned the night before the big test. Students were even given the option of taking the test in whichever classroom they felt most at ease. The day of the test, all students were treated to a free snack of bagels and juice.

The school achieved exemplary test scores, which were announced in the newspapers (showing comparisons to other schools), and teachers were involved in at least three additional celebrations (a sort of pep rally for the teachers). The entire school faculty attended a special banquet at a nearby luxury hotel, joined by school board members and administrators. The teachers were thanked for their hard work and congratulated by all. Pictures from the banquet were published in the newspaper. Officials from the State Department of Public Instruction, accompanied by local school board members, addressed the entire school at an assembly, at which a special banner was hung outside the building proclaiming the school as a School of Excellence. The following year at a systemwide assembly, the teachers were recognized with balloons for their school's achievement.

This school's efforts and the time dedicated to preparation for testing are echoed around the country as schools take up the challenge of high-stakes accountability (e.g., Nolan, Haladyna, and Haas, 1992; Smith, 1991). In Virginia, for example, the superintendent of one district decided to frame testing as a sports event by giving students and teachers the challenge of beating the neighboring rival school district (Bracey, 1996). The students, when asked what they were going to do on the tests, chanted out "Beat (the neighboring) county!" The school held pep rallies where students who had to take the test were cheered on by those students who were not required to take the test. In one Pennsylvania school, the school announcements included a song sung to the tune of "High Hopes" (Rothman, 1996, p. 29):

> We have worked and studied so long,
> Hope we don't get anything wrong
> As you have probably guessed,
> On the test
> We'll do our very best
> 'Cause we've got high hopes

Teachers engage in test preparation to ensure that parents and students are aware of the high stakes involved in the test. Their actions are motivated by a series of factors including a desire for their students to do well on the test, a competitive interest in making sure their school and class scores are high relative to others, a fear of being embarrassed by low scores, an interest in receiving salary bonuses and public recognition, and a desire to gain a measure of control over externally mandated testing.

But equally important is a critical analysis of the *time* that is spent engaged in these types of motivational activities. In the example of the middle school described previously, at least seven sessions of a student advisory program were dedicated to test preparation. Time in each content area classroom was given to advising students on preparing for the test. An entire day of instruction was geared to motivating students to do well on the test. Teachers spent time at parent conferences, spent time at a parent-teacher open house, and used instructional planning time preparing for the motivational sessions. All of these test preparation activities took place in addition to teaching to the test, practicing for the test, and the actual time given for students to take the test.

As a result of these practices, time is taken away from classroom instruction. As one principal explained, the accountability tests take "time away from meaningful learning for kids and meaningful instructional tasks for teachers. It takes a week for the test and thirty to forty-five minutes per day in the six weeks preceding the tests" (Mitchell, 1997, p. 263).

PRACTICING FOR THE TESTS

In a survey of North Carolina's teachers, 80 percent of elementary teachers reported that they spent more than 20 percent of their total teaching time practicing for high-stakes tests (Jones et. al, 1999). Even more dismaying was that 28 percent of teachers reported spending more than 60 percent of their time practicing for the state's tests. When asked if this was more or less time than in years prior to testing, 71 percent of the teachers said that they spent more time practicing for the high-stakes tests.

In another study conducted by Shepard and Doughtery (1991), more than one-third of the teachers studied spent more than two weeks giving students old forms of standardized tests for practice. Smith (1991) found that as testing approached, teachers increased their test preparation as the reality of the stakes of the test became imminent. In another survey of teachers and students (Public Agenda, 2001), 83 percent of teachers indicated concern that teaching to the test could become the norm, and 20 percent of responding students felt that their teachers focused so much on test preparation that "real learning" was neglected.

Principals often put pressure on teachers to spend time preparing students for the test. "One principal told his teachers not to introduce new material in the six weeks before the test; this time was to be spent on review, especially in formats used in the upcoming exam" (Perreault, 2000, p. 706). Similarly, Smith (1991) interviewed elementary teachers in Arizona and found that 80 percent of the teachers were encouraged to raise scores on the Iowa Test of Basic Skills, and 32 percent said that they were "required" to do test preparation with students. In addition, 28 percent of the Arizona teachers surveyed said they begin their test preparation at least two months before the test administration.

Why not practice for the tests? From the perspective of the teacher, practicing for the test provides students with the knowledge and skills they need to perform well on the test. The benefits of this preparation seem enormous: students score higher, teachers and administrators receive recognition, and the community rejoices that their school is better than others. Moreover, as the North Carolina state superintendent responded when asked about the large amounts of time teachers spend practicing for the tests, "If teachers are focusing in large part on the tests, this means they're focusing on the state curriculum" (Cenziper, 1998).

A cursory examination of the issue would suggest that if the test is an accurate sample of the curriculum, and teachers are teaching to the test, then teachers must be teaching to the curriculum. This would appear to be exactly what should happen: students learning the knowledge and skills included in the curriculum. In fact, test preparation *can* focus teachers and students on specific knowledge and skills. However, the use of test preparation can also invalidate the interpretation of the test scores. In the following sections, we will explore how test preparation affects how test scores can be interpreted.

Item Teaching

What does it mean when teachers report spending a lot of time practicing for tests? It likely means different things to different teachers, but we will consider one specific instance here. When the Jones et al. (1999) survey was being developed, the researchers asked teachers and administrators how they interpreted the following survey item: "How much time per year do your students spend practicing for the end-of-grade tests?" The teachers said that they interpreted "practicing" as giving students instruction and materials that would be similar to those that would appear on the test. Teachers in other studies have reported similar methods of preparing for tests. For instance, Perreault (2000) reported:

"Teachers noted that there was less essay work done, and that required writing often took the formats tested on state exams" (p. 707).

These descriptions of practicing fall into Popham's (2000a) definition of "item teaching." Specifically, teaching to a test's items includes "teachers who organize their instruction, for instance, teacher-explained illustrative items or items-based practice activities—either around the actual items found in a test or around a set of look-alike items" (Popham, 2000a, p. 2). An example of a look-alike type of teaching would be as follows: a teacher knows that multiplication problems such as "2 x 14 = what?" will appear on students' tests, so the teacher gives students problems such as "What is 4 times 12?" Teaching the broader domain of multiplication is appropriate, but teaching only look-alike items is problematic.

Standardized tests are designed to assess only a sample of what a student knows from a larger range of knowledge and skills. A sample is necessary because given time and monetary constraints, it is generally impossible to create a test that assesses all of the knowledge and skills that most curriculum standards require. To do so would require longer tests that generally take students more time to complete and cost more to develop, administer, and score. Given these practical considerations, the tests measure only a small range of the knowledge and skills specified in the curriculum standards.

Popham (2000b) suggests that a simple way to think about the content domain and test sample is to draw a circle and fill it with several X-marks. The area inside the circle is the curriculum content domain that represents the knowledge and skills that the students are supposed to know. For instance, it could represent the knowledge and skills students are supposed to know about social studies in the fifth grade. Since there is generally too much knowledge and too many skills to measure in one testing session (especially considering the amount of time that a fifth grader can be expected to sit for a test), a sample of this domain is used. The sample is represented by the X-marks, each of which represents a test item. For instance, one X-mark might represent the item, "What year did Columbus come to America?"

The foundation of testing rests on the ability to make an accurate inference from students' scores on a test to their wider understandings of the content domain. The problem with item teaching is that students learn the knowledge and skills tested, but not the other knowledge and skills in the domain. In relation to the previous example, they would learn the X-marks, but not the knowledge and skills between the X-marks within the circle. "Frequently, standardized achievement tests try to do their assessment job with only 40–50 items per subject field, sometimes fewer" (Popham, 2000b, p. 396). As a result, these items might query low-level knowledge that has limited value in teaching students critical thinking and the wider range of skills needed to be successful in later life (Suarez and Gottovi, 1992). Item teaching is a serious abuse of testing and cheats students out of the opportunity to gain other knowledge and skills in the content domain.

In contrast to item teaching, curriculum teaching is instruction directed toward a specific domain of content knowledge or skills: "Curriculum-teaching . . . refers to the aiming of a teacher's instruction at test-represented content rather than at test items" (Popham, 2000a, p. 2). Curriculum teaching falls within the range of ethical behavior (Mehrens and Kaminski, 1989; Linn, 2000); teachers teach the curriculum that will be tested, without narrowly teaching *only* those items that will be tested.

But there is a large gray area between teaching the curriculum domain that will be tested and teaching the specific items that will be tested. For example, the curriculum may call for students to be able to calculate percentages. One teacher may give the students problems such as: "What is 30 percent of 80?" Another teacher may ask students: "Calculate the sale price of an $80.00 pair of shoes when there is a 30 percent sale." In another case, the teacher may ask students to measure their height in meters and figure out how the height of the dinosaur at the local museum compares to their height. Each of these teachers is teaching about percentages, but the level of complexity differs in each case. It is possible that the teacher who asked his or her students to calculate percentages in the form of "What is 30 percent of 80?" will have students who score very well when asked these kinds of problems on a test. However, the teacher who is asking his or her students to consider the relative heights of dinosaurs and humans will find himself or herself teaching more than the tested objectives of percentages but also teaching about measurement; the metric system; bipedal and quadrupedal skeletons; and potentially about topics such as evolution, surface area, and extinction.

Many educators believe that teachers should simply teach, using what they believe to be good instruction (such as the teacher who taught percentages within the rich context of relative heights) without teaching to the test, and have faith that the test scores will reflect students' knowledge and skills (Canner, 1992). If test development had evolved to the sophisticated level that quality teaching has, then teachers who teach the general curriculum would have students with test scores that reflect the richness of students' learning. But given our current low levels of test development, the teacher who narrowly focuses on tested topics of the curriculum is likely to see test scores as high or higher than the scores of the teacher who teaches the general curriculum. The critical problem is that tests often fail to measure the complexity of learning that takes place in schools. This discrepancy between what is taught and what is tested leaves teachers feeling cheated and undermined by a failing accountability system.

We must ask whether it is realistic to expect teachers to provide quality teaching when so much emphasis is placed on increasing test scores. This emphasis is magnified when schools adopt any of the many test preparation materials now available to teachers. In fact, one of the consequences of high-stakes testing is the development of a whole industry that produces and sells test preparation materials that promote item teaching. Commercially prepared practice tests are exploding in abundance as states engage in more and more testing. These materials are geared to assist teachers in preparing students specifically for the content of high-stakes tests. For example, teachers can buy books with practice tests such as "Ohio Science Proficiency Review: Preparing for Your Exit Level Test" (Cohen, Deutsch, and Sorrentino, 2000) or "Preparing for TAAS: Mathematics, Exit Level with Answers" (Dustrhoff, 1998). One publisher sells specific grade-level test preparation materials for Florida, Georgia, Massachusetts, Michigan, New Jersey, North Carolina, Ohio, and Texas. The Internet is also emerging as a major vehicle for the delivery of test preparation materials for students' use in and out of school (Rothman, 2001). In two studies of Arizona teachers' test preparation practices, Smith (1991) and Nolen, Haladyna, and Haas (1992) found that at least 40 percent of teachers used commercial test preparation materials.

Inflated Scores

One of the more interesting phenomena to take place in American educational history is the Lake Wobegon effect (Koretz, 1988), which emerged after a physician noticed that nearly every state and most school systems reported that their students were scoring above average on standardized, nationally norm-referenced tests. The "Lake Wobegon Report" issued in 1987 asserted that all states reporting statewide test scores ranked above the national average (Cannell, 1987). The fact that more than half the states scored above the average reflects a tendency for test scores to rise after repeated use of the same test.

Linn (2000) reported that test scores on norm-referenced tests rise due to a variety of factors that have little to do with real change in the students being tested. This phenomenon is known as the saw-tooth effect: when a new form of a test is introduced, scores are typically low for a couple of years, then they steadily rise until a new form of the test is introduced. To the naïve observer, the increase in scores appears to indicate that students are learning more and that the quality of education is rising. But this increase in scores is often the result of a narrow focusing of instruction on the skills and question types used on the tests. Linn argues that "common sense and a great deal of hard evidence indicate that focused teaching to the test encouraged by accountability uses of results produces inflated notions of achievement when results are judged by comparison to national norms" (Linn, 2000, p. 7).

One of the more recently publicized examples of this phenomenon came from students' scores on the Texas Assessment of Academic Skills (TAAS) tests. Students' reading and math TAAS scores had improved so dramatically over a few years that the score gains had been called the "Texas miracle." A team of researchers from RAND (a nonprofit research institution) investigated this large increase in test scores to determine whether the scores accurately reflected students' increased achievement (Klein, Hamilton, McCaffrey, and Stecher, 2000). To do so, they compared fourth and eighth grade students' TAAS scores to scores on another test, the National Assessment of Educational Progress (NAEP). The NAEP tests reflect standards endorsed by a national panel of experts and are considered one of the best indicators of student achievement in the country. Interestingly, Texas students' scores on the NAEP tests increased much less than they had on the TAAS. In fact, the increases in the NAEP scores were no greater than the increases reported nationally, with the exception of the fourth grade NAEP math test (on which the Texas students did improve significantly more than students nationwide).

How could the TAAS scores show such a dramatic increase in reading and math achievement and the NAEP tests show such a small increase? The RAND researchers explained the difference between the test scores as follows:

> The large discrepancies between TAAS and NAEP results raise serious questions about the validity of the TAAS scores. We do not know the sources of these differences. However, one plausible explanation, and one that is consistent with some of the survey and observation results cited earlier, is that many schools are devoting a great deal of class time to highly specific TAAS preparation. (Klein, Hamilton, McCaffrey, and Stecher, 2000)

In other words, one explanation is that teachers were able to better prepare students for the TAAS tests each year because they knew more about the format and content of the questions on the TAAS tests each year. (The TAAS test questions were made public after the exam was administered each year.) Thus, while students' scores might have been increasing on the TAAS tests due to the *specific* test preparation for these tests, students' scores were not increasing as rapidly on the NAEP tests that assessed more general content knowledge and problem solving skills. As a result, the reported increase in achievement might have been more a reflection of test preparation than actual increased learning or deep understanding of the content domain.

Test Score Pollution

The fact that some schools likely spend more time practicing for the tests than they did before the testing program began leads to "test score pollution." Test score pollution refers to the "unequal and uncontrolled variety of test preparation and test administration practices that contaminate all comparisons among schools because students did not have the same opportunities to perform on the test" (Urdan and Paris, 1994, p. 139). Consider students at a school that did not have pep rallies, free bagels and juice, test-taking strategy sessions, and instruction geared toward specific items, as described for the middle school in the previous example. Comparing the test scores of students without the test preparation to the students with these additional preparations is invalid because the former students had an unfair advantage. As Haladyna, Nolen, and Haas (1991, p. 4) reason: "pollution increases or decreases test performance without connection to the construct represented by the test, producing construct-irrelevant test score variance." In other words, compared to students with similar knowledge and skills at another school, the students at the middle school described previously might have scored higher due to factors other than their knowledge and skills.

Narrowing the Curriculum

As we discussed in chapter 2, another problem with test preparation is that teachers often spend more time teaching subjects that are tested. Because many state tests include only reading, writing, and mathematics, other subjects included in the curriculum such as science, social studies, music, art, physical education, and health receive less attention. If teachers are strictly gearing their instruction toward reading, writing, and mathematics, they have less time to teach the other parts of the curriculum. This lack of congruence between what is tested and what is supposed to be taught according to the curriculum standards creates tension, because some areas of the curriculum become privileged over others. Canner (1992) states: "spending a great deal of instructional time teaching to the specific objectives included on the test, to the exclusion of other content, is inappropriate" (p. 10).

THE ETHICS OF TEST PREPARATION

Unethical Test Preparation

Test preparation strategies fall along an ethical continuum from unethical to ethical test preparation strategies (Haladyna, Nolen, and Haas, 1991). Examples of inappropriate test preparation have appeared in nearly every state that has implemented high-stakes testing. For instance, in South Carolina a teacher was fired for breaching test security by giving test questions and answers to students several days before the official test was administered (Canner, 1992). The teacher said that her goal was to help her low-achieving students.

In Columbus, Ohio, a fifth grade teacher was reprimanded for the low scores of her students. The principal wanted to know why that teacher's students didn't do as well as they had in previous years. So, the teacher asked her students about their scores this year and in previous years. Their response was, "Well . . . that's because they gave us the answers and you didn't" (Mathews and Argetsinger, 2000, p. A1). According to the *Washington Post*, this teacher was later forced out of teaching because she complained about coaching by teachers who had administered the previous year's proficiency exam.

In Montgomery County, Virginia, an elementary school principal resigned after parents protested the fact that students were assisted in rewriting answers to essay questions and were pointed toward correct answers on the test (Mathews and Argetsinger, 2000). In Austin, Texas, a deputy superintendent was charged with increasing school scores after school administrators changed identification numbers of low-achieving students whose scores they didn't want counted in the report (Mathews and Argetsinger, 2000).

There are also less obvious ways of cheating on tests, such as when at-risk students, English as a second language students, or students with learning disabilities are not included in testing. There have been cases of some students being told that it would be acceptable for them to stay home on the day of testing (e.g., Barksdale-Ladd and Thomas, 2000). Another dramatic way to circumvent low test scores is to encourage low-achieving students to drop out of school, and thus eliminate their scores from the school's ranking completely (Merrow, 2001).

Cheating on high-stakes tests has led to the development of whole new strategies for catching those who bend the rules. There are now computer programs designed to count erasures on tests. The number of erasures on a set of tests for a class or school is compared to the number of erasures found on the tests for other classes or schools. Too many erasures are viewed as a signal that someone is tampering with the tests. In Chicago, middle school students were required to retake the Iowa Test of Basic Skills after an administrator allegedly changed answers and filled in incomplete tests. Michael Kean, a vice president for CTB/McGraw-Hill (a test development company) admits that "the higher the stakes, the more likely there is going to be some problem" (Mathews, 2000, p. C08).

To prevent unethical practices, school systems use a variety of measures to protect test integrity. In many schools, there are outside test monitors who must be present for the duration of the test. Test booklets are carefully counted, sealed, and monitored along every point in the distribution system. Typically, teachers are not allowed to see the test items until they are placed in the hands of the students. Directions are usually scripted so that each test proctor is required to say the same words. But there are a number of gray areas that raise concerns for teachers. What if a teacher sees a student start to fill in answers on the wrong section of the answer sheet? Should the teacher be allowed to redirect the student? What about stray marks on an answer sheet? For a test-savvy high school student, most would agree that stray marks should stand; but what about a third grader who barely holds a fat pencil upright? Should a teacher make a comment if a child is marking more than one answer per question? These examples highlight the differences in goals of a testing program that seeks valid, reliable scores and those of the classroom teacher who knows her students well and wants them to at least have a fighting chance of scoring well.

The pressure for teachers to raise scores is enormous and comes from all sides of educational arenas. A survey of teachers conducted by Shepard and Doughtery (1991) found that teachers feel substantial pressure to raise test scores, pressure that comes from parents (17 percent), other teachers (24 percent), principals (56 percent), the media (66 percent), and district-level administrators and school boards (79 percent). When teachers serve children who come from areas of high poverty, have large numbers of students with learning disabilities, or have classes with non-English-speaking students, the challenges and pressures to raise scores are significant.

When cheating occurs, who is to blame? According to Monty Neill, with the National Center for Fair and Open Testing, the blame rests with tests and not teachers. "The major problem is the unreasonable, unfair, and inappropriate use of standardized exams" (Kleiner, 2000, p. 1). The high stakes associated with tests creates a school culture intent on raising scores at all costs. Neill argues, "the only way to stop [cheating] is to return tests to their appropriate role, not as an absolute determinate [*sic*] of kids' progress but as one source of information, to be judged in conjunction with things like grades and teachers' judgments" (Kleiner, 2000, p. 2). The sad reality of cheating and high-stakes tests is that these actions influence children and teach them unintended lessons about politics, ethics, honesty, and character.

Ethical Test Preparation

Is it ever appropriate to prepare students for tests? Yes. Ethical uses of test preparation include teaching students generic test-taking strategies. This includes helping students understand how to read the directions and questions carefully, regulate testing time, identify item distracters and context cues, identify guessing strategies, and check their answers (Linn and Gronlund, 1995). Helping students understand how to take tests and how to maximize responses so that the tests more accurately reflect their knowledge is useful.

But how many times does a student need to be taught test-taking skills? And when does teaching test-taking strategies go beyond teaching generic skills that are applicable in a variety of testing contexts, to the point of inappropriate instruction that is designed to teach specific items? Again, the high stakes of testing ensure that educators will teach test-taking skills to make sure that their students do well. But stepping back from the short-term gain of test-taking skills, one has to ask to what degree our children need to know how to determine whether guessing is worthwhile or how to fill in bubbles on an answer sheet.

TEST PREPARATION: HOW MUCH IS TOO MUCH?

There is a growing concern that educators are putting too much emphasis on testing and test preparation. Parent John Sery pulled his child out of school during a week of testing after he saw how much time was being used in test preparation. According to Sery, "It was time that could be better utilized. I think it really stresses the kids out" (Trejos, 2000, p. C01).

Preparing students for tests that are the gateways for college and graduate school seems a worthwhile goal. Teachers want students to be comfortable taking tests, able to read and answer a test with intelligent strategies, and able to complete a computerized answer sheet with ease. But after a brief introduction to test-taking skills, educators at all levels struggle with issues of test preparation. Where do we draw the line between test preparation and the unintended goal of education for testing?

By stepping away from the narrow view of testing, we can begin to look systematically at the role of testing in education. Is a week too much for test preparation? How about two weeks? If a school is in session for 180 school days, is it too much to take one day per week to prepare for tests? This is exactly what one elementary school in North Carolina does. Every Friday, Carrie, a first grade teacher, leaves her class with a worksheet and a teacher assistant and joins all the other teachers in her school to work one-on-one with students who are at risk of failing the end-of-grade test for fourth graders. For the fourth grade student who is at risk, the extra help may be a huge benefit. But what about the class of twenty-five first graders who are left without a teacher? Don't those students also deserve the best education available, even if there isn't testing for them at the end of the school year? Would those fourth grade students be at risk if they had received quality instruction during grades 1–3? Is one day per week too much?

Taking a macroscopic view of testing also raises questions about motivational activities. Should teachers and students be taken away from the limited time they have for teaching and learning to engage in activities designed to raise awareness of the importance of testing? What would be taking place if teachers weren't engaging in test preparation with students? If instructional time was being wasted, then the loss of time for test preparation may be negligible. But if teachers used all their instructional time for high-quality teaching and learning, then the time used for test preparation might prove to be a large hole where student learning is lost.

CONCLUSION

In this chapter, we have explored the unintended consequences of test preparation for high-stakes assessment. There is evidence that teachers and students spend considerable time engaged in a wide variety of test preparation activities. Teachers are teaching increasing amounts of test-taking strategies and skills. Students are involved in motivational activities designed to heighten their awareness of the high stakes associated with test scores. Time within the school day is being shifted away from nontested subjects and focused on those areas that are tested. Teachers, in many cases, are involved in item teaching and are limiting their instruction to only those types of learning activities that are directly tested.

The high stakes associated with testing have resulted in a myriad of unethical test preparation strategies, including some that would be defined as cheating. Instances of cheating are being increasingly reported for teachers, principals, and school district administrators. Although one goal of high-stakes assessment is to raise student achievement, there is growing evidence that this goal is undermined by narrowly focused test preparation that takes considerable time and resources from the limited school day.

Popham (2000a) questions whether we can control inappropriate test preparation: "Because teaching to a test's items, or to clone-like replicas of those items, eviscerates the validity of score-based inferences, whether those inferences are made by teachers, parents, or policymakers, item-teaching is reprehensible. It should be stopped. But can it be?" (p. 3). As long as the stakes are high and as long as educators' jobs are at risk, it is likely that schools will pursue any means possible to raise test scores.

REFERENCES

Barksdale-Ladd, M., and K. Thomas. 2000. "What's at Stake in High-Stakes Testing: Teachers and Parents Speak Out." *Journal of Teacher Education* 51, no. 5, 384–97.

Bracey, G. 1996. "Altering the Motivation in Testing." *Phi Delta Kappan* 78, no. 3, 251–52.

Cannell, J. J. 1987. *Nationally Normed Elementary Achievement Testing in America's Public Schools: How All Fifty States are Above the National Average* (2nd ed.). Daniels, W.V.: Friends of Education.

Canner, J. 1992. "Regaining the Public Trust: A Review of the School Testing Programs, Practices." *NASSP Bulletin* 76, 6–15.

Cenziper, D. 1998. "Teachers Denounce ABCs Testing, Poll Says." *Charlotte Observer*, 11 August, 7C.

Cohen, P., J. Deutsch, and A. Sorrentino. 2000. *Ohio Science Proficiency Review: Preparing for Your Exit Level Test*. New York: Amsco.

Dustrhoff, M. 1998. *Preparing for TAAS: Mathematics, Exit Level with Answers.* New York: Amsco.

Haladyna, T., S. Nolen, and N. Haas. 1991. "Raising Standardized Achievement Test Scores and the Origins of Test Score Pollution." *Educational Researcher* 20, no. 5, 2–7.

Jones, M. G., D. Jones, B. Hardin, L. Chapman, T. Yarbrough, and M. Davis. 1999. "The Impact of High-Stakes Testing on Teachers and Students." *Phi Delta Kappan* 81, no. 3 (November), 199–203.

Klein, S. P., L. S. Hamilton, D. F. McCaffrey, and B. M. Stecher. 2000. *What Do Test Scores in Texas Tell Us?* www.rand.org/publications/electronic/ed.html (accessed 11 April).

Kleiner, C. 2000. "Test Case: Now the Principal's Cheating." *U.S. News On-Line,* 12 June. www.usnews.com/usnews/issue/000612/cheating.htm (accessed 11 April 2002).

Koretz, D. 1988. "Arriving at Lake Wobegon: Are Standardized Tests Exaggerating Achievement and Distorting Instruction?" *American Educator* 12, no. 2, 8–15, 46–52.

Linn, R. 2000. "Assessments and Accountability." *Educational Researcher* 29, no. 2, 4–16.

Linn, R. L., and N. E. Gronlund. 1995. *Measurement and Assessment in Teaching.* Englewood Cliffs, N.J.: Prentice Hall.

Mathews, J. 2000. "As Stakes Rise, Even Erasures Count on Tests: Scrutiny Intensifies as Cheating Alleged on Standardized Exams." *Washington Post,* 4 June, C08.

Mathews, J., and A. Argetsinger. 2000. "Cheating on Rise Along with Testing: Teachers Complain of Pressure to Do Well on Standardized Exams." *Washington Post,* 2 June, A1.

Mehrens, W., and J. Kaminski. 1989. "Methods for Improving Standardized Test Scores: Fruitful, Fruitless, or Fraudulent?" *Educational Measurement: Issues and Practices* 8, 14–22.

Merrow, J. 2001. "Undermining Standards." *Phi Delta Kappan* 82, no. 9, 652–59.

Mitchell, K. J. 1997. "What Happens when School Reform and Accountability Testing Meet?" *Theory into Practice* 36, 262–65.

Nolen, A., T. Haladyna, and N. Haas. 1992. "Uses and Abuses of Achievement Test Scores." *Educational Measurement: Issues and Practices* 11, no. 2, 9–15.

Perreault, G. 2000. "The Classroom Impact of High-Stress Testing." *Education* 120, no. 4, 705–10.

Popham, W. J. 2000a. "Teaching to the Test: High Crime, Misdemeanor, or Just Plain Good Instruction." Paper presented at the American Educational Research Association annual meeting, New Orleans, 24–28 April 2000.

Popham, W. J. 2000b. *Modern Educational Measurement.* Boston: Allyn and Bacon.

Public Agenda. 2001. *Reality Check.* www.publicagenda.org/specials/rc2001/reality .htm (accessed 11 April 2002).

Rothman, B. 2001. "School Testing Bandwagon Spawns Web Coaching Sites." *New York Times,* 24 May, G6.

Rothman, R. 1996. "Taking Aim at Testing." *American School Board Journal* 183, no. 2, 27–30.

Shepard, L., and K. Doughtery. 1991. "Effects of High-Stakes Testing on Instruction." Paper presented at the annual meeting of the American Educational Research Association, Chicago, 3–7 April. (ERIC Document Reproduction Service No. ED 337 468).

Smith, M. L. 1991. "Meanings of Test Preparation." *American Educational Research Journal* 28, no. 3, 521–42.

Suarez, T., and N. Gottovi. 1992. "The Impact of High Stakes Assessments in Our Schools." *NASSP Bulletin* 76, no. 545, 82–88.

Trejos, N. 2000. "Some Students Sitting out the MSPAPs." *Washington Post*, 7 May, C01. Also at washingtonpost.com/wp-dyn/articles/A19378–2000May6.html (accessed 11 April 2002).

Urdan, T. C., and S. G. Paris. 1994. "Teachers' Perceptions of Standardized Achievement Tests." *Educational Policy* 8, no. 2, 137–56.

Chapter Five

Testing and Student Motivation

I've seen [my] two children, a seventh and ninth grader, who initially loved school and were so motivated and enthusiastic now hate it. My son last year didn't quite understand the Amish people, but he heard that they only go to school through the eighth grade, so he begged to move to Pennsylvania so he could quit. (Yarbrough, 1999, p. 79)

Although there has been much discussion about how high-stakes tests affect students' learning and achievement, there has been less discussion about how testing affects students' academic *motivation*. Yet, fostering students' motivation (i.e., active engagement in learning) and promoting lifelong learning are among the many important goals of public education. Some believe that high-stakes tests motivate students to achieve their potential. Yet, others have found evidence to the contrary. For instance, when asked whether the "TAAS [Texas Assessment of Academic Skills] motivates students to learn," on average, educators indicated that it does not (Hoffman, Assaf, and Paris, 2001). Data such as these suggest that high-stakes tests are not useful as motivators.

The purpose of this chapter is to further investigate this issue by focusing on how high-stakes tests affect students' academic motivation. This chapter is not intended to provide a comprehensive review of all of the research and motivation theories that might affect students' academic motivation, because several other books provide this information (e.g., Brophy, 1998; Pintrich and Schunk, 2002; Reeve, 1996; Stipek, 1998). Rather, we have attempted to include some of the major research and theories that are most relevant to examining student motivation within a high-stakes testing environment. To do so, we provide a theoretical background along with research studies that have examined the effects of high-stakes tests on students' motivation. Some brief suggestions for how teachers can increase students' motivation are also provided.

INTRINSIC VERSUS EXTRINSIC
MOTIVATION

One of the most common and intuitive beliefs about motivation is that students are more likely to be motivated to choose an activity and persist at it if they enjoy the activity and are interested in it. Researchers have defined this type of motivation as intrinsic motivation because students participate in an activity simply for its own sake (Pintrich and Schunk, 2002). That is, intrinsically motivated students enjoy or are interested in their work. On the other hand, extrinsically motivated students complete tasks to receive rewards such as a grades or prizes.

Researchers have found that intrinsic motivation facilitates learning and achievement (Gottfried, 1985). For instance, the result of one study found a correlation between students' intrinsic motivation and their self-reported comprehension and actual recall of the material (Ryan, Connell, and Plant, 1990). On the other hand, extrinsic motivation has been associated with a number of negative outcomes, such as a higher likelihood of dropping out of school (Vallerand and Bissonnette, 1992); student anxiety (Ryan and Connell, 1989); lower creativity (Amabile, 1983); and less flexible thinking (McGraw and McCullers, 1979). Because of the many positive outcomes related to intrinsic motivation and the negative outcomes related to extrinsic motivation, it makes sense for schools to strive to intrinsically motivate students.

Extrinsic Rewards

High-stakes tests reward students who pass the tests by allowing them to move on to the next grade. Often, rewards and prizes are also given to students for improved test scores. Students who fail the tests are not rewarded, but rather may suffer consequences such as attending summer school or repeating the grade. Early studies on the effects of extrinsic rewards on students' intrinsic motivation have shown that providing rewards for an activity decreases students' intrinsic motivation for that activity (Deci, 1971; Lepper, Greene, and Nisbett, 1973). Furthermore, intrinsic motivation decreases in the presence of other external events that are experienced as controlling, such as evaluations (Smith, 1974), threats of punishment (Deci and Cascio, 1972), imposed goals (Mossholder, 1980), competition (Deci, Betley, Kahle, Abrams, and Porac, 1981), and deadlines (Amabile, DeJong, and Lepper, 1976). Based on this research, we can predict that high-stakes tests may decrease students' intrinsic motivation, because they are an evaluation of students' ability, there are threats of punishment (low-achieving students are retained), there are imposed goals (students must meet the standards at their grade level), it is often seen as a competition between schools (and possibly students, classes, and districts), and there are deadlines (students must learn the content material by the date that the high-stakes test is given). These studies suggest that students may be *less* intrinsically motivated in schools that give high-stakes tests because of the controlling aspects of external events. A parent shared the following about his second grade daughter:

> The main focus of the school is getting ready for the test. They still enjoy music, art, and PE [physical education], but the kids know that the test is the real thing and they all think something will happen to them if they don't pass it. Even my daughter, who is a good student, worries about it needlessly. What a life for an eight year old.

This account shows that even a second grader is aware of the extrinsic motivation involved with testing.

To compound the effects of extrinsic rewards, some schools provide high-achieving students with other rewards and prizes in addition to the reward of passing the test. For instance, one school provided limousine rides for students who scored at the highest level and new bicycles for students who showed the greatest improvement (George, 2001). A principal in another state reported, "If [the students] try hard, I give them an ice cream or pizza party afterwards" (Firestone and Mayrowetz, 2000, p. 728). Another administrator promised to shave his head if students scored well on the high-stakes tests (George, 2001). True to his word, he followed through on the promise. The school board of another district with low test scores "seriously contemplated using cash incentives for students but did not do so" (Firestone and Mayrowetz, 2000, p. 728). These types of extrinsic rewards are common in schools today, due in part to the high-stakes testing environment.

Unfortunately, there have been few studies that have measured the impact of high-stakes tests on students' motivation directly. Instead, many of the studies have queried teachers about how they perceive the effects of high-stakes tests on students' motivation. Some of these studies are discussed in the next section.

Intrinsic Motivation

In one study, 1,324 teachers were asked how the state's high-stakes testing program had affected students' "love of learning" (Yarbrough,

1999). While teachers might have interpreted the phrase "love of learn-ing" to have different meanings, one likely interpretation is that students whose love of learning has been positively affected would enjoy learning more and be more intrinsically motivated to learn with the addition of high-stakes tests. Conversely, students whose love of learning was nega-tively affected would likely enjoy learning less and be less intrinsically motivated: 41.4 percent of the teachers reported that the high-stakes testing program "negatively" affected students' love of learning, com-pared to 6.4 percent who reported that the program "positively" affected students' love of learning. The remaining 52.2 percent of teach-ers indicated that there was no effect on students' motivation. Therefore, teachers' overall perception of the effect of high-stakes testing on stu-dents' motivation is not favorable; many teachers reported that it decreased motivation, while fewer reported positive effects.

A reduction in intrinsic motivation was also reported by teachers in British Columbia, who found that students were so focused on the high-stakes graduation test that they "tuned out" if they knew that what was being discussed in class was not going to be on the test (Wideen et al., 1997). These students were clearly not interested in the subject matter itself; rather, they were concerned with the extrinsic reward of passing the test.

The tests can also limit the options teachers have available to them to intrinsically motivate students. One teacher blamed the tests for reduc-ing "the number of unusual and interesting things [she was] able to do" (Wideen et al., 1997, p. 438). Another teacher noted:

> Before, you know, I could just go with the kids if something came up which hooked them. But now if we just start off in a different direction, I get worried we won't get back to what's required, and I have to kind of rein them in. I know they get frustrated, and I sure do. (Perreault, 2000, p. 707)

When the test does not cover topics that the teacher finds personally interesting, teachers report: "students miss the enthusiasm and energy that the teacher brings to these topics" (Wideen et al., 1997, p. 438).

These studies suggest that when high-stakes tests are used as rewards for students, the result is likely to be a decrease in students' intrinsic motivation.

INTRINSIC MOTIVATION AND
SELF-DETERMINATION THEORY

Thus far, we have assumed that the high-stakes tests or prizes associated with them affect students' intrinsic motivation directly. In other words, students perceive their passing high-stakes tests as a reward. However, there are other factors that might mediate the effects of high-stakes tests on students' motivation. As Deci and Ryan (1994) pointed out, "although certain events tend, on average, to be either controlling or autonomy supportive, the *style and language* with which the events are administered significantly influence their effects" (emphasis added, p. 8). This conclusion was based on studies such as Ryan, Mims, and Koestner's (1983) study, which found that administering performance-contingent rewards in a controlling style (e.g., "perform well, as you *should*") undermined intrinsic motivation, while administering rewards in an autonomy-supportive style was less likely to undermine intrinsic motivation. "When limits were set without using pressuring language and in a way that provided choice and acknowledged feelings, they were not detrimental to intrinsic motivation" (Deci and Ryan, 1994, p. 8). The results of these studies indicate that teachers have an effect on students' intrinsic motivation. Consequently, we must consider not only how students interpret the pressures of high-stakes tests, but also, how teachers interpret the pressures of high-stakes tests.

In this section, we describe self-determination theory to provide a theoretical background for how high-stakes tests might affect teachers' teaching styles. Deci and Ryan (1985, 1991) have proposed a theory of self-determination that postulates that basic psychological needs are inherent in human life. Deci and his colleagues assume an organismic perspective in that individuals have needs from the time they are born and these needs evolve with development. Self-determination involves having the ability to make choices and being able to manage the interaction between oneself and the environment. An individual who is self-determined will "engage in an activity with a full sense of wanting, choosing, and personal endorsement" (Deci, 1992, p. 44).

Self-determination theory specifies three innate psychological needs that relate to intrinsically motivated processes: autonomy, competence, and relatedness (Deci and Ryan, 1985). Autonomy refers to an individual's control over his or her actions. An autonomous individual wants to perform the activity and have control over his or her actions during an activity. On the other hand, a controlled individual may intend to achieve an outcome but may lack a true sense of choice. Autonomy can only occur when one's actions emanate from within oneself and are one's own (Deci and Ryan, 1987). The second psychological need, competence, involves an individual's knowledge of how to accomplish an outcome as well as his or her ability to perform the actions to achieve the outcome. Lastly, relatedness encompasses an individual's attempts to develop secure and satisfying relations with others. Deci and Ryan (1991) "believe these three innate psychological needs are reasonably exhaustive and help to explain a substantial amount of variance in human behavior and experience" (p. 243).

How do these three needs relate to intrinsic motivation? "Simply stated, social–contextual factors that afford people the opportunity to satisfy their needs for autonomy, competence, and relatedness will facilitate intrinsic motivation" (Deci and Ryan, 1994, p. 7). The implication of self-determination theory for educators is that teachers' social interactions with students and the activities that they provide to them can either support or diminish students' intrinsic motivation. For instance, students are more intrinsically motivated when they are able to choose which tasks to engage in and decide how much time to allot for each (Swann and Pittman, 1977; Zuckerman et al., 1978).

In short, self-determination theory states that individuals have the need to be in control of their actions (autonomous); be good (competent) at what they do; and have secure and satisfying relationships with others. As a result, students will be intrinsically motivated when they have control of their actions, feel competent, and develop satisfying relationships with others. The next section provides some of the specific research that has been conducted to develop self-determination theory.

Autonomy-Supportive versus Controlling Teachers

Several researchers have studied teachers' social interactions with students by comparing the effects of "autonomy-supportive" teachers versus "controlling" teachers on students' intrinsic motivation (Deci and Ryan, 1987). For example, Deci, Schwartz, Sheinman, and Ryan (1981) assessed teachers' orientations toward autonomy versus control in their interactions with students and found that students of teachers who were more autonomy-oriented were more intrinsically motivated than students of teachers who were more control-oriented. The students in these classes were also aware of the effects of their teachers' orientation, as students' perceptions of their classroom climate correlated with their teachers' orientation. Similar results were obtained by other researchers, who found that students who perceived their teachers to be autonomy-oriented reported higher levels of intrinsic motivation than students who perceived their teachers to be control-oriented (Ryan and Grolnick, 1986; Vallerand, 1991).

Other researchers have labeled self-determined students as "origins" because their behavior originates from their own needs, thoughts, feelings, and desires (deCharms, 1976). In contrast, students were labeled as "pawns" if they felt controlled by external forces in their environment. Students of teachers who were more autonomy-supportive became less pawnlike and more originlike (deCharms, 1976).

In addition to being more intrinsically motivated, students of autonomy-supportive teachers and originlike students have been shown to reap other benefits, including enhanced conceptual learning (Benware and Deci, 1984; Boggiano et al., 1993; Flink, Boggiano, and Barrett, 1990; Grolnick and Ryan, 1987); greater perceived academic and social competence (Deci, Schwartz, Sheinman, and Ryan, 1981; Ryan and Grolnick, 1986); a higher sense of self-worth (Harter, 1982; Ryan and Grolnick, 1986) and self-esteem (Deci, Schwartz, Sheinman, and Ryan, 1981); greater creativity (Amabile, 1979, 1985; Amabile, Hennessey, and Grossman, 1986); a preference for challenging tasks (Boggiano, Main, and Katz, 1988; Shapira, 1976); a more positive emotional tone (Csikszentmihalyi, 1985; Ryan and Connell, 1989); and increased school attendance (deCharms, 1976; Vallerand and Bissonnette, 1992).

Why are there so many positive outcomes of autonomy-supportive teaching? Teachers who are more autonomy-supportive help to fulfill students' need to be in control of their learning, while controlling teachers take away students' choices and autonomy.

Effects of High-Stakes Tests on Autonomy Support

With all of the positive outcomes associated with autonomy-supportive teachers and originlike student behavior, it is important to consider how high-stakes tests affect teachers' autonomy support and students' origin beliefs. Thus, the question addressed in this section is: Can teachers create an autonomy-supportive classroom that fosters students' originlike behavior within the context of a high-stakes testing environment? That is, is it realistic to expect teachers to behave in an autonomy-supportive manner when they are surrounded by administrators, parents, and others who place pressure on them to ensure that students perform up to standards?

Studies have shown that when teachers are pressured to increase students' performance, they become less autonomy-supportive and more controlling (Flink, Boggiano, and Barrett, 1990). As an example, when teachers were asked to teach students about spatial relation puzzles, teachers responded differently when their goal was to focus on student

learning as compared to when they were pressured to have students perform up to standards (Deci, Spiegel, Ryan, Koestner, and Kauffman,
1982). An experimental design was set up in which teachers in the "non-
pressured" condition were told, "Your role is to facilitate the student's
learning how to work with the puzzles. There are no specific performance requirements; your job is simply to help the student learn to solve
the puzzles" (p. 853). Other teachers were in a "pressured" condition
and were told, "Your role is to ensure that the student learns to solve
the puzzles. It is a teacher's responsibility to make sure that students perform up to standards. If for example, your student were tested on the
puzzles, he (or she) should be able to do well" (p. 853). Teachers in the
pressured condition talked more, used more controlling strategies, gave
students much less choice, and let students solve fewer puzzles on their
own.

The results of these studies suggest that if high-stakes tests make
teachers feel pressured and responsible for ensuring that their students
perform up to standards, the teachers will be more controlling. As a
result, the students will be less likely to experience all of the positive outcomes described previously for students who are more originlike and
who are taught by autonomy-supportive teachers.

To assess the effects of these types of studies within the context of
high-stakes testing, Jones et al. (1999) surveyed teachers about whether
they felt more pressured and responsible as a result of high-stakes tests.
Elementary teachers in North Carolina (where the high-stakes testing
program is called the "ABCs") were asked to answer the following question on a seven-point Likert scale (this scale allowed teachers to choose
a number from one to seven and provided the following descriptors at
numbers one, four, and seven: 1 = much less stressful; 4 = no change;
7 = much more stressful): "Since the ABCs program was adopted, how
much more or less stressful is your job?" The mean response value was
6.2 (more stressful)—0.4 percent of the teachers selected a value of 1, 2,
or 3 (less stressful), 10.6 percent of the teachers selected a value of 4 (no
change), and 88.9 percent of the teachers selected a value of 5, 6, or 7
(more stressful). More than half of the teachers (55.7 percent) selected a
value of 7 (much more stressful).

Teachers were also asked to rate the following question on a similar
seven-point Likert scale (1 = much less responsible; 4 = no change; 7 =
much more responsible): "Since the ABCs program was adopted, how
much more or less responsible do you feel for your students' performing
up to standards?" The mean response value was 5.6 (more responsible)—1.3 percent of the teachers selected a value of 1, 2, or 3 (less

responsible), 28.6 percent of the teachers selected a value of 4 (no change), and 70.1 percent reported a value of 5, 6, or 7 (more responsible). About one-third (33.8 percent) selected a value of 7 (much more responsible). These findings suggest that the high-stakes testing program made most teachers feel more stressed and more responsible for students' performing up to standards. The implication is that teachers will likely respond in a similar way as the teachers in the pressured group in the Deci et al. (1982) and Flink et al. (1990) studies and become more controlling towards their students.

Other studies have also found that teachers feel pressure as a result of the testing. Barksdale-Ladd and Thomas (2000) reported that the teachers they interviewed felt constant pressure and stress to ensure high scores on their state test. As one teacher noted, "The pressure is on. I feel pressure, partly from the constant memos. I internalize the pressure, and it is always with me" (p. 390). Similarly, Perreault (2000) found that teachers reported that the pressure of the state testing program, whether direct or indirect, was always present. One teacher stated, "The first thing they told us this year was when the testing would be done. We were told to put those dates in our plan books and work back from there" (p. 706). Another teacher reported, "Now it's like you're always being observed and you know there is something they want to see and it like pushes on you all the time and I resent it, I really do" (p. 707). Teachers in British Columbia, where there is a mandatory high-stakes graduation examination, also reported feeling psychological pressures associated with the high-stakes exam (Wideen et al., 1997). As a teacher of grades ten and twelve stated: "So you have got that pressure there and it changes how you function as a human being if you've got this thing where everybody is going to be looking at you, how your results are" (Wideen et al., 1997, p. 438). Obviously, the teachers cited in these studies felt pressured to make their students perform up to standards.

Although we have found no empirical research to demonstrate whether high-stakes testing makes teachers less autonomy-supportive and more controlling, there is plenty of evidence that high-stakes tests make teachers feel more pressure and responsibility for students to meet the standards. Based on motivation theories that have been empirically tested, we can infer that it is likely that high-stakes tests make teachers more controlling; and as a result, students may become less intrinsically motivated.

Fostering an Autonomy-Supportive Environment in the Classroom. Because high-stakes tests are likely to foster a controlling style of teaching, this section focuses on how teachers can create an autonomy-supportive classroom that fosters student autonomy and originlike behavior. Based on the results of several research studies (e.g., Deci, Connell, and Ryan, 1989; Deci, Eghrari, Patrick, and Leone, 1994; Koestner et al., 1984), Reeve (1996) developed a list of teaching behaviors that support students' autonomous behavior. "The first step in supporting students' autonomy is to minimize the use of superfluous social controls" (Reeve, 1996, p. 28). After the superfluous controls are removed, teachers can promote students' autonomy and self-determination by:

1. understanding and appreciating students' points of view,
2. encouraging students' choices and initiatives,
3. communicating the rationale for any behavioral limits or constraints placed on students,
4. acknowledging that negative emotion is a valid reaction to teacher control,
5. communicating in a noncontrolling style and providing positive feedback. (Reeve, 1996)

Interestingly, all five of these teaching behaviors can be accomplished within the pressures of high-stakes testing. Consequently, it is *possible* for teachers to be autonomy-supportive in a high-stakes testing environment. Given all of the pressure associated with high-stakes testing, however, it seems unlikely that the tests have helped teachers to become more autonomy-supportive. As researchers have noted, "We are speculating that performance standards may not be inherently antagonistic to intrinsic motivation (of teachers and students), although when teachers or students experience them as pressure, they are likely to [become more controlling]" (Deci et al. 1982, p. 858).

As a final note, it is important to acknowledge that autonomy-supportive teachers *do* have rules and limits. As Reeve (1996) notes, "autonomy support is *not* permissiveness run amuck" (p. 36). Instead, autonomy-supportive teachers impose structure and have rules and limits but do so in a manner that is informational and noncontrolling rather than coercive and controlling. One way teachers can do this is by explaining the rationale behind rules such as "no talking" (Deci and Ryan, 1985); another is to provide students with a limited range of choices that have been deemed acceptable by the teacher.

Competence

In addition to autonomy, competence is one of the three innate human psychological needs according to self-determination theory (Deci and

Ryan, 1985). We all have the need to be competent; that is, we all want to interact effectively with our environment. Feedback provides objective performance information that allows us to evaluate whether we are effective and competent. Feedback in school comes from a variety of sources including the task itself, students' comparisons of current performances with past performances, and evaluations from others. Research indicates that positive feedback that increases perceived competence also increases intrinsic motivation (Deci et al., 1991). On the other hand, negative feedback tends to decrease perceived competence and intrinsic motivation (Deci, Cascio, and Krusell, 1973; Vallerand and Reid, 1984). Interestingly, research indicates that an increase in intrinsic motivation only occurs when the feedback is accompanied by support for autonomy (Fisher, 1978; Ryan, 1982). As Deci and Ryan (1994) note, "the feelings of competence must be accompanied by perceived autonomy in order for one to be intrinsically motivated" (p. 9).

What are the implications of this research showing that students have a need for competence? High-stakes tests provide a source of feedback about a student's ability that could increase students' perceived competence and level of intrinsic motivation if they pass the test. However, this could only be true if it is also assumed that students' autonomy was supported (as discussed in the previous paragraph). Similarly, students who failed a high-stakes test would have a lower perceived competence and lower level of intrinsic motivation. One teacher's comment exemplifies this perspective:

> It kills them when they flunk it. And putting them in the TAAS [Texas Assessment of Academic Skills] remediation class is considered a slap. They consider it extra work. They're probably already doing bad on it (TAAS-related content) in the classroom, and so now they consider this (TAAS remediation) a punishment. (Gordon and Reese, 1997, p. 357)

High-stakes tests can also adversely affect students' intrinsic motivation when the high-stakes tests are not consistent with the feedback students were given from their teachers. For instance, if a student was a capable writer and had high perceived competence in writing based on his teachers' feedback, and he subsequently failed a high-stakes writing test, his perceived competence would likely decrease along with his intrinsic motivation. A study by Gordon and Reese (1997) found as follows: "Many of the teachers lamented that they had worked hard to build up at-risk students' self-concepts and help them to achieve some measure of academic success, only to have the students' progress wiped out by the TAAS failure" (p. 357).

Of course, the opposite is also true. If a student with a low perceived competence (based on her teachers' feedback) passed the writing test, she would likely experience an increase in her perceived competence and intrinsic motivation. As a result, it is difficult to predict the effect of a high-stakes test on a student's perceived competence because it depends upon many factors including a student's existing level of perceived competence, the quality and accuracy of the teacher's feedback, and the reliability and validity of the high-stakes test.

The few studies that have specifically assessed the effects of high-stakes tests on students' competence have shown somewhat mixed results. Jones et al. (1999) surveyed teachers about their perceptions of students' confidence by asking: "Which of the following student characteristics do you attribute to the ABCs program?" Forty percent of the teachers attributed a change in students' confidence to the high-stakes testing program, with 24.3 percent reporting that students were less confident and 15.4 percent reporting that students were more confident. The fact that nearly one-quarter of the teachers believed that students were less confident is significant because individuals with less confidence (i.e., self-efficacy) have been shown to be less motivated; that is, they set lower goals (Locke and Latham, 1990, 1994; Zimmerman and Bandura, 1994), choose easier tasks (Sexton and Tuckman, 1991), and exert less effort and persist for a shorter time at tasks (Bandura and Cervone, 1983, 1986; Bouffard-Bouchard, 1990; Zimmerman, 1995).

On the other hand, some teachers have reported that since the start of the testing, students' motivation increased. Many attributed this change to the fact that they were more aware of their students' skill levels and were doing a better job of providing students with experiences that matched their skill level, resulting in more success for students (Jones and Johnston, 2002). Successful students were seen as more motivated students, which is consistent with current motivation theories.

Fostering Competence in the Classroom. There are several things that teachers can do to foster students' academic competence. First, teachers should allow students to be successful at academic tasks. Teachers can accomplish this by providing students with optimally challenging tasks that match their skills (Csikszentmihalyi, 1990). Teachers can also provide students with verbal feedback that informs them that their performance is competent (Vallerand and Reid, 1984). In doing so, teachers should create a classroom climate that tolerates students' failures and allows them to challenge themselves by taking risks (Clifford, 1990).

Relatedness

The third innate need cited by Deci and Ryan (1985) is relatedness. A student's need for relatedness is satisfied through genuine interpersonal involvement with parents and teachers. Denying young children involvement with adults has been shown to decrease children's intrinsic motivation (Anderson, Manoogian, and Reznick, 1976). Moreover, parents who were more involved with their children and provided autonomy support tended to have children who were more intrinsically motivated and self-determined (Grolnick and Ryan, 1989). Thus, relatedness facilitates intrinsic motivation when accompanied by autonomy-supportive contexts.

The implication of Grolnick and Ryan's study for high-stakes testing is that if parents and teachers are more involved in a child's life, the child should be more intrinsically motivated. Unfortunately, we found no studies that measured whether parents and teachers were more involved in their child's life as a result of high-stakes tests. Instead, we have only seen a mixture of anecdotal evidence. For instance, we have spoken to a few teachers who claimed that parents were more involved in their child's schooling as a result of the high-stakes testing program. Having the parents more involved with their child should lead to a higher level of intrinsic motivation for the child. However, a teacher's quote in another study would lead us to believe that the tests have hindered relationships between teachers and students:

> Our children are hurting more than ever. If there was ever a time to change, it is now. Give teachers back their classrooms. Let them teach and spend quality time with their students. They need us! (Hoffman, Assaf, and Paris, 2001, p. 491)

We cannot reach any definitive conclusions about how relatedness has been affected by high-stakes testing programs without further studies in this area.

Fostering Relatedness in the Classroom. Teachers can foster relatedness in the classroom by developing sincere quality relationships with their students. Teachers might do so by showing an interest in students, caring about students, and/or dedicating their time and energy to students (Connell, 1990; Connell and Wellborn, 1991).

GOAL THEORIES

Goal orientation theory is another motivation theory that can be used to examine the effects of testing on students' motivation. This theory examines why and how students approach and engage in achievement tasks (Pintrich and Schunk, 2002). Similar to the intrinsic and extrinsic orientations described previously, goal orientations can be divided into

mastery and performance goals. In some ways, mastery goals are comparable to intrinsic motivation and performance goals are comparable to
extrinsic motivation. "A *mastery goal* orientation is defined in terms of
a focus on learning, mastering the task according to self-set standards or
self-improvement, developing new skills, improving or developing competence, trying to accomplish something challenging, and trying to gain
understanding or insight" (Pintrich and Schunk, 2002, p. 214). "A *performance goal* orientation, in contrast to a mastery orientation, represents a focus on demonstrating competence or ability and how ability
will be judged relative to others, for example, trying to surpass normative performance standards, attempting to best others, using social comparative standards, striving to be the best in the group or class on a task,
avoiding judgments of low ability or appearing dumb, and seeking public recognition of high performance levels" (Pintrich and Schunk, 2002,
pp. 214, 216).

Students who focus on learning and mastering a task are said to have
an "approach" mastery goal, whereas students who avoid learning or
mastering the task have an "avoidance" mastery goal. Similarly, students who focus on being the best and smartest in comparison to others
have an "approach" performance goal and students who focus on avoiding looking stupid have an "avoidance" performance goal (Pintrich and
Schunk, 2002, p. 219).

In general, researchers have found students with *mastery* goal orientations to be more engaged in learning than students with *avoidance* performance goal orientations. For instance, in comparison with students
with avoidance performance goals, students with mastery goals have
been found to be more interested in tasks (Rawsthorne and Elliot, 1999);
be more likely to self-monitor their learning and check their understanding (Ames and Archer, 1988); use more effective learning strategies
(Meece, Blumenfeld, and Hoyle, 1988); and be more likely to seek help
when needed for learning (Newman, 1994). Furthermore, "students
who are oriented to avoiding negative judgments of their competence
are clearly more anxious about tests and their performance (Middleton
and Midgley, 1997; Skaalvik, 1997)" (Pintrich and Schunk, 2002,
p. 224).

The research on how mastery goal orientations compare to *approach*
performance goals is more difficult to interpret. In many ways, students
with approach performance goals appear to reap many of the same benefits as students with mastery goals, such as high self-efficacy (Wolters et
al., 1996); increased interest and enjoyment (Harackiewicz et al., 1998);
and the use of more effective learning strategies (Wolters, Yu, and Pin-

trich, 1996). In fact, recent studies have found that students with approach performance goals actually score higher on achievement measures than those with mastery goals (Elliot, McGregor, and Gable, 1999; Harackiewicz et al., 1997, Harackiewicz, Barron, and Elliot, 1998).

Implications of Goal Theories

What are the implications of goal theories as related to high-stakes testing? It's impossible to predict exactly how high-stakes testing affects students' motivation because, as discussed previously, it depends upon how the pressures of the tests are interpreted by teachers and students. We can, however, consider how testing may generally affect teachers and students. High-stakes testing fosters a performance goal orientation in that it places the focus of schooling on judging a student's ability relative to a normative standard and uses social comparisons as a means of recognition. Standardized testing does not foster a mastery goal orientation in which the focus is on improving or developing according to self-set standards.

Some students likely develop an approach performance orientation in which they are successful on the tests and continue to want to be the best and brightest. For these students, the tests positively affect their motivation, as they will work hard to remain the best. It would be interesting to know how many of these students were already successful in school and were already motivated prior to the advent of high-stakes testing. Our guess is that many of these students were already successful in school.

Others who score poorly on the tests and/or fail will likely develop an avoidance performance orientation. With regards to student motivation, the greatest negative unintended consequence of the testing is that these students adopt an avoidance performance orientation and focus on not failing and not looking stupid. For these students, the tests negatively affect their motivation, and consequently, their learning. Ms. Kent, a third grade teacher, tells a story about one of her students who appears to have adopted an avoidance performance orientation:

> He cried when he didn't pass the level test. He doesn't get the results he should from the amount of effort he puts in. He becomes more withdrawn as he realized his own disability and is less willing to write. He doesn't want to put things on paper, as he is afraid it is going to look bad. (Fu and Lamme, 2002, p. 247)

We must question whether testing is educating a generation of lifelong learners with a mastery goal orientation, or a generation of test takers whose main motivation is to score well or avoid scoring poorly on tests.

Clearly, more research needs to be conducted to measure how testing has affected students' goal orientations. Until then, we can get some sense of how testing is affecting students' goal orientations by examining students' level of anxiety. Students with an *avoidance* performance orientation tend to be more anxious about their performance on tests than students with an *approach* performance orientation (Middleton and Midgley, 1997; Skaalvik, 1997; Wolters, Yu, and Pintrich, 1996). In the following section, we discuss the effects of high-stakes tests on students' stress and anxiety.

STUDENTS' STRESS AND ANXIETY

The North Carolina Association of Educators found that 63 percent of teachers and administrators reported that the focus on testing had added to students' level of stress (Elliott, 2000). Consistent with this finding, 61.2 percent of the teachers in another survey attributed student anxiety to high-stakes tests (Jones et al., 1999). Other studies have found the percentage of teachers reporting that students showed signs or symptoms of stress to be as high as 83 percent (Adams and Karabenick, 2000). One teacher described the pressure students feel as follows:

> I see so much anxiety. We are seeing ulcers diagnosed in younger children, we're seeing panic attacks, more kidney infections. I have children who won't use the restroom all day. They are afraid to miss class time unless it's a class break. They will not ask to go individually because they don't want to miss something in the classroom. (Yarbrough, 1999, pp. 79–80)

When teachers in Texas were asked about the effects of high-stakes tests on their students, they reported a range of student stress levels. Some students were totally indifferent about the tests, other students experienced moderate stress, and other students experienced high levels of stress (Gordon and Reese, 1997). Gordon and Reese found that students who experienced high levels of stress could be categorized into one of three subgroups:

> For some of the students in [the high stress] group, the stress they experience leads to anxiety and even panic as the test draws near. For a second subgroup, the stress leads to anger and resentment. A third subgroup eventually responds

to the stress by "shutting down"; they cope by telling themselves they have no chance of doing well on the TAAS and giving up. (p. 356)

In general, high anxiety has been show to have detrimental effects on student performance. For instance, students with higher levels of anxiety in achievement situations perform worse (Everson, Smodlaka, and Tobias, 1994; Pintrich and de Groot, 1990); have less effective study skills (Neveh-Benjamin, McKeachie, and Lin, 1987; Topman, Kleijn, van der Ploeg, and Masset, 1992); are more prone to using avoidance as a coping strategy (Blankstein, Flett, and Watson, 1992; Zeidner, 1994); are distracted easily when learning new material (Dusek, 1980; Eysenck, 1991); and worry about their performance to such an extent that it interferes with their ability to retrieve and demonstrate knowledge and skills (Zatz and Chassin, 1985; Tobias, 1986, 1992).

Another method to assess students' level of stress and anxiety is to look at their physical symptoms. To do so, researchers surveyed Texas educators who reported that while taking the Texas Assessment of Academic Skills (TAAS), students experienced stomachaches and headaches and that they were anxious, irritable, or aggressive (Hoffman, Assaf, and Paris, 2001). These educators reported that 32 percent of students "often" experienced an upset stomach and that 53 percent "sometimes" experienced an upset stomach. Further, educators said 14 percent "always" experienced headaches, 33 percent "often" experienced headaches, and 45 percent "sometimes" experienced them.

In an interesting study of students in Massachusetts, researchers asked teachers to have their fourth, eighth, and tenth grade students "Draw a picture of yourself taking the MCAS [Massachusetts Comprehensive Assessment System]" (Wheelock, Bebell, and Haney, 2000). They categorized the drawings into groups and found that more drawings depicted negative affective responses to the testing than depicted positive responses. In drawings that showed a *general* positive or negative response to the test, they found 19.3 percent of drawings to convey negative responses (e.g., "I hate MCAS"; "This test is stupid") compared to only 2.9 percent of drawings that were positive (e.g., "I had fun"). Other drawings showed more distinct personal attitudes and feelings, so the researchers grouped these drawings into more specific categories. Negative responses were grouped into categories such as anxiety (13.4 percent of drawings; see figure 5.1); anger (10 percent of drawings; see figure 5.2); sleeping or daydreaming (5.3 percent of drawings); boredom (4.9 percent of drawings); relief that testing had ended (3.9 percent of drawings); sadness (2.7 percent of drawings); and anticipating failure, grade retention, or a poor score (2.2 percent of drawings). Positive responses included diligent and motivated test takers (18 percent of drawings), thinking or problem solving (7.3 percent of drawings; see figure 5.3), and confidence (5.4 percent of drawings; see figure 5.4).

As a whole, these data reveal that students are feeling the pressure of the tests and that some students are more affected than others.

CONCLUSION

The important question to ask is not whether students are motivated, but rather, what type of motivation do they have? Are they intrinsically or extrinsically motivated? Do they have a mastery goal orientation or an avoidance performance orientation? Do they enjoy school subjects and focus on learning, or are they motivated by rewards and afraid to fail the tests?

Figure 5.1   "Pressure, stress, anxiety, dull"

Figure 5.2 From top to bottom: (1) "I hate the M-CAST I want to throw it in the trash"; (2) "Oh man this really stinks"; (3) "and badly"; (4) "I hate school i don't want to go"; (5) "why dose it have to be me!"

Figure 5.3 "THINK!"

Figure 5.4 "A+"

High-stakes testing environments promote a climate that encourages short-term achievement gains over long-term intrinsic motivation. As one study found: "Many school leaders focus first on making a quick breakthrough in student achievement. They want immediate, concrete results that can be measured by better test scores" (George, 2001, p. 28). While this appears to be a noble goal, it is often accomplished with extrinsic rewards that might motivate students in the short term but that undermine students' long-term intrinsic motivation. This point is often misunderstood and therefore deserves emphasis. It is possible for high-stakes tests to be used as a reward to increase motivation in the short term. However, extrinsic rewards have been shown to decrease intrinsic motivation in the long term when perceived to be controlling. As a result, students might enjoy school subjects less in the future even though they appear to be more motivated (extrinsically by rewards) in the short term. Recent research has supported this prediction, as teachers have reported that high-stakes tests have decreased students' love of learning (intrinsic motivation) and increased their level of stress and anxiety.

We have presented evidence in this chapter that students are more intrinsically motivated when they are taught by autonomy-supportive teachers. Moreover, when teachers are pressured to increase students' performance, they become less autonomy-supportive and more controlling. We predicted that high-stakes tests will pressure teachers to become more controlling and less autonomy-supportive; and as a result, students' intrinsic motivation may decrease. In fact, several studies have indicated that teachers felt more pressured as a result of high-stakes testing. This finding leads us to believe that these teachers would also be more controlling and that their students would be less intrinsically motivated. These findings are consistent with Deci, Vallerand, Pelletier, and Ryan's (1991) conclusion: "Government agencies, parent groups, and other forces outside the school system bring pressure to bear on school administrators and teachers alike, and all of these intrusions on the teachers' sense of self-determination are likely to lead them to be more controlling with their students. That, in turn, will have negative effects on the students' self-determination, conceptual learning, and personal adjustment" (p. 340).

We also reviewed research pertaining to how high-stakes tests affect students' competence and relatedness needs. We have found much less research in these areas; therefore, it is difficult to make generalizations about how high-stakes tests might affect students' intrinsic motivation through a change in their competence or relatedness.

While we cannot definitively conclude that high-stakes tests lower students' intrinsic motivation, the preponderance of evidence leads us to believe that high-stakes tests are more likely to lower students' intrinsic motivation than to raise it. This finding is supported by both theory and empirical research. To provide more conclusive evidence of the effects of high-stakes tests on students' motivation, more research needs to be conducted within specific contexts (classrooms and schools) and specific high-stakes testing programs (at the district or state level).

Finally, we provided evidence that some students have higher levels of stress and anxiety as a result of the testing. High anxiety has detrimental effects on students' performance and might also indicate that these students have adopted avoidance performance goal orientations. This evidence suggests that testing has had a negative effect on some students' motivation.

This chapter reminds us that schooling is about more than simply gathering facts and obtaining knowledge; it is also about enjoying the process of learning and having the opportunity to explore new knowledge. Too often, testing programs focus on cognitive development without considering the implications on students' emotional and social development. As one teacher stated:

> In the past we were all concerned for the whole child, we wanted our children to be well balanced, and I could tell which children were lacking in social skills and which children needed to learn to get along with each other. I could zoom in on all the different problems, not just academic problems. But now it's become [so that] nothing is important but the test. It's not important if it's not on the test, and I think we are losing sight, we're burying children with these test scores. (Yarbrough, 1999, p. 79)

The next two chapters examine this issue further by describing how testing affects special populations and students who are retained.

REFERENCES

Adams, L., and S. A. Karabenick. 2000. "Impact of State Testing on Students and Teaching Practices: Much Pain, No Gain?" Paper presented at the meeting of the American Educational Research Association, New Orleans, April.

Amabile, T. M. 1979. "Effects of External Evaluations on Artistic Creativity." *Journal of Personality and Social Psychology* 37, 221–33.

Amabile, T. M. 1983. *The Social Psychology of Creativity.* New York: Springer.

Amabile, T. M. 1985. "Motivation and Creativity: Effect of Motivational Orientation on Creative Writers." *Journal of Personality and Social Psychology* 48, 393–99.

Amabile, T. M., W. DeJong, and M. R. Lepper. 1976. "Effects of Externally Imposed Deadlines on Subsequent Intrinsic Motivation." *Journal of Personality and Social Psychology* 34, 92–98.

Amabile, T. M., B. A. Hennessey, and B. S. Grossman. 1986. "Social Influence on Creativity: The Effects of Contracted-for Rewards." *Journal of Personality and Social Psychology* 50, 14–23.

Ames, C., and J. Archer. 1988. "Achievement Goals in the Classroom: Students' Learning Strategies and Motivation Processes." *Journal of Educational Psychology* 80, 260–67.

Anderson, R., S. T. Manoogian, and J. S. Reznick. 1976. "The Undermining and Enhancing of Intrinsic Motivation in Preschool Children." *Journal of Personality and Social Psychology* 34, 915–22.

Bandura, A., and D. Cervone. 1983. "Self-Evaluative and Self-Efficacy Mechanisms Governing the Motivational Effects of Goal Systems." *Journal of Personality and Social Psychology* 45, 1017–28.

Bandura, A., and D. Cervone. 1986. "Differential Engagement of Self-Reactive Influences in Cognitive Motivation." *Organizational Behavior and Human Decision Processes* 38, 92–133.

Barksdale-Ladd, M. A., and K. F. Thomas. 2000. "What's at Stake in High-Stakes Testing: Teachers and Parents Speak Out." *Journal of Teacher Education* 51, 384–97.

Benware, C. A., and E. L. Deci. 1984. "Quality of Learning with an Active versus Passive Motivational Set." *American Educational Research Journal* 21, no. 4, 755–65.

Blankstein, K., G. Flett, and M. Watson. 1992. "Coping and Academic Problem-Solving Ability in Test Anxiety." *Journal of Clinical Psychology* 48, 37–46.

Boggiano, A. K., C. Flink, A. Shields, A. Seelbach, and M. Barrett. 1993. "Use of Techniques Promoting Students' Self-Determination: Effects on Students' Analytic Problem-Solving Skills." *Motivation and Emotion* 17, 319–36.

Boggiano, A. K., D. S. Main, and P. A. Katz. 1988. "Children's Preference for Challenge: The Role of Perceived Competence and Control." *Journal of Personality and Social Psychology* 54, 134–51.

Bouffard-Bouchard, T. 1990. "Influence of Self-Efficacy on Performance in a Cognitive Task." *Journal of Social Psychology* 139, 353–63.

Brophy, J. 1998. *Motivating Students to Learn*. Boston: McGraw Hill.

Clifford, M. M. 1990. "Students Need Challenge, Not Easy Success." *Educational Leadership* 48, 22–26.

Connell, J. P. 1990. "Context, Self, and Action: A Motivational Analysis of Self-System Processes across the Life-Span." In *The Self in Transition: From Infancy to Childhood*, ed. D. Cicchetti, p. 61–97. Chicago: University of Chicago Press.

Connell, J. P., and J. G. Wellborn. 1991. "Competence, Autonomy, and Relatedness: A Motivational Analysis of Self-System Processes." In *Self-Processes in Development: Minnesota Symposium on Child Psychology* (vol. 23), ed. M. R. Gunnar and L. A. Sroufe, 167–216. Hillsdale, N.J.: Lawrence Erlbaum.

Csikszentmihalyi, M. 1985. "Reflections on Enjoyment." *Perspectives in Biology and Medicine* 28, 469–97.

Csikszentmihalyi, M. 1990. *Flow: The Psychology of Optimal Experience.* New York: Harper and Row.

deCharms, R. 1976. *Enhancing Motivation: Change in the Classroom.* New York: Irvington.

Deci, E. L. 1971. "Effects of Externally Mediated Rewards on Intrinsic Motivation." *Journal of Personality and Social Psychology* 18, 105–15.

Deci, E. L. 1992. "The Relation of Interest to the Motivation of Behavior: A Self-Determination Theory Perspective." In *The Role of Interest in Learning and Development*, ed. K. A. Renninger, S. Hidi, and A. Krapp, 43–70. Hillsdale, N.J.: Erlbaum.

Deci, E. L., G. Betley, J. Kahle, L. Abrams, and J. Porac. 1981. "When Trying to Win: Competition and Intrinsic Motivation." *Personality and Social Psychology Bulletin* 7, no. 1, 79–83.

Deci, E. L., and W. F. Cascio. 1972. "Changes in Intrinsic Motivation as a Function of Negative Feedback and Threats." Paper presented at the Meeting of the Eastern Psychological Association, Boston, April.

Deci, E. L., W. F. Cascio, and J. Krusell. 1973. "Sex Differences, Verbal Reinforcement, and Intrinsic Motivation." Paper presented at the meeting of the Eastern Psychological Association, Washington, D.C., May.

Deci, E. L., J. P. Connell, and R. M. Ryan. 1989. "Self-Determination in a Work Organization." *Journal of Applied Psychology* 74, 580–90.

Deci, E. L., H. Eghrari, B. C. Patrick, and D. R. Leone. 1994. "Facilitating Internalization: The Self-Determination Theory Perspective." *Journal of Personality* 62, 119–42.

Deci, E. L., and R. M. Ryan. 1985. *Intrinsic Motivation and Self-Determination in Human Behavior.* New York: Plenum.

Deci, E. L., and R. M. Ryan. 1987. "The Support of Autonomy and the Control of Behavior." *Journal of Personality and Social Psychology* 53, 1024–37.

Deci, E. L., and R. M. Ryan. 1991. "A Motivational Approach to Self: Integration in Personality." *In Nebraska Symposium on Motivation: Vol. 38, Perspectives on Motivation*, ed. by R. Dienstbier. Lincoln: University of Nebraska Press.

Deci, E. L., and R. M. Ryan. 1994. "Promoting Self-Determined Education." *Scandinavian Journal of Educational Research* 38, no. 1, 3–14.

Deci, E. L., A. J. Schwartz, L. Sheinman, and R. M. Ryan. 1981. "An Instrument to Assess Adults' Orientation toward Control versus Autonomy with Children: Reflections on Intrinsic Motivation and Perceived Competence." *Journal of Educational Psychology* 73, 642–50.

Deci, E. L., N. H. Spiegel, R. M. Ryan, R. Koestner, and M. C. Kauffman. 1982. "The Effects of Performance Standards on Teaching Styles: The Behavior of Controlling Teachers." *Journal of Educational Psychology* 74, 852–59.

Deci, E. L., R. J. Vallerand, L. G. Pelletier, and R. M. Ryan. 1991. "Motivation and Education: The Self-Determination Perspective." *Educational Psychologist* 26, no. 3 and 4, 325–46.

Dusek, J. 1980. "The Development of Test Anxiety in Children." In *Test Anxiety:*

Theory, Research, and Applications, ed. I. Sarason, 87–110. Hillsdale, N.J.: Lawrence Erlbaum.

Elliot, A. J., H. McGregor, and S. Gable. 1999. "Achievement Goals, Study Strategies, and Exam Performance: A Mediational Analysis." *Journal of Educational Psychology* 91, 549–63.

Elliott, J. 2000. *NCAE: ABCs Accountability Statement* (17 July). www.ncae.org/news/000717pr.shtml (accessed 23 July 2000).

Everson, H., I. Smodlaka, and S. Tobias. 1994. "Exploring the Relationship of Test Anxiety and Metacognition on Reading Test Performance: A Cognitive Analysis." *Anxiety, Stress and Coping: An International Journal* 7, 85–96.

Eysenck, M. 1991. "Anxiety and Attention." In *Anxiety and Self-Focused Attention*, ed. R. Schwarzer and R. A. Wicklund, 125–31. New York: Harwood Academic.

Firestone, W. A., and D. Mayrowetz. 2000. "Rethinking 'High Stakes': Lessons from the United States and England and Wales." *Teachers College Record* 102, no. 4, 724–49.

Fisher, C. F. 1978. "The Effects of Personal Control, Competence and Extrinsic Reward Systems on Intrinsic Motivation." *Organizational Behavior and Human Performance* 21, 273–88.

Flink, C., A. K. Boggiano, and M. Barrett. 1990. "Controlling Teaching Strategies: Undermining Children's Self-Determination and Performance." *Journal of Personality and Social Psychology* 59, no. 5, 916–24.

Fu, D., and L. L. Lamme. 2002. "Assessment through Conversation." *Language Arts* 79, no. 3, 241–50.

George, P. S. 2001. "A + Accountability in Florida?" *Educational Leadership* 59, no. 1, 28–32.

Gordon, S. P., and M. Reese. 1997. "High-Stakes Testing: Worth the Price?" *Journal of School Leadership* 7, 345–68.

Gottfried, A. E. 1985. "Academic Intrinsic Motivation in Elementary and Junior High School." *Journal of Educational Psychology* 77, 631–45.

Grolnick, W. S., and R. M. Ryan. 1987. "Autonomy in Children's Learning: An Experimental and Individual Difference Investigation." *Journal of Personality and Social Psychology* 52, no. 5, 890–98.

Grolnick, W. S., and R. M. Ryan. 1989. "Parent Styles Associated with Children's Self-Regulation and Competence in School." *Journal of Educational Psychology* 81, no. 2, 143–54.

Harackiewicz, J., K. Barron, S. Carter, A. Letho, and A. Elliot. 1997. "Determinants and Consequences of Achievement Goals in the College Classroom: Maintaining Interest and Making the Grade." *Journal of Personality and Social Psychology* 73, 1284–95.

Harackiewicz, J., K. Barron, and A. Elliot. 1998. "Rethinking Achievement Goals: When Are They Adaptive for College Students and Why?" *Educational Psychologist* 33, 1–21.

Harter, S. 1982. "The Perceived Competence Scale for Children." *Child Development* 53, 87–97.

Hoffman, J. V., L. C. Assaf, and S. G. Paris. 2001. "High-Stakes Testing in Reading: Today in Texas, Tomorrow?" *The Reading Teacher* 54, no. 5, 482–92.

Jones, B. D., and A. F. Johnston. 2002. "The Effects of High-Stakes Testing on Instructional Practices." Paper presented at the 2002 annual meeting of the American Educational Research Association, New Orleans, April.

Jones, G. M., B. D. Jones, B. H. Hardin, L. Chapman, T. Yarbrough, and M. Davis. 1999. "The Impact of High-Stakes Testing on Teachers and Students in North Carolina." *Phi Delta Kappan* 81, 199–203.

Koestner, R., R. M. Ryan, F. Bernieri, and K. Holt. 1984. "Setting Limits on Children's Behavior: The Differential Effects of Controlling versus Informational Styles on Intrinsic Motivation and Creativity." *Journal of Personality* 52, 233–48.

Lepper, M. R., D. Greene, and R. E. Nisbett. 1973. "Undermining Children's Intrinsic Interest with Extrinsic Rewards: A Test of the 'Overjustification' Hypothesis." *Journal of Personality and Social Psychology* 28, 129–37.

Locke, E., and G. Latham. 1990. *A Theory of Goal Setting and Task Performance.* Englewood Cliffs, N.J.: Prentice Hall.

Locke, E., and G. Latham. 1994. "Goal Setting Theory." In *Motivation: Theory and Research*, ed. H. O'Neil and M. Drillings, 13–29. Hillsdale, N.J.: Lawrence Erlbaum.

McGraw, K. O., and J. C. McCullers. 1979. "Evidence of a Detrimental Effect of Extrinsic Incentives on Breaking a Mental Set." *Journal of Experimental Social Psychology* 25, 285–94.

Meece, J., P. C. Blumenfeld, and R. H. Hoyle. 1988. "Students' Goal Orientation and Cognitive Engagement in Classroom Activities." *Journal of Educational Psychology* 80, 514–23.

Middleton, M., and C. Midgley. 1997. "Avoiding the Demonstration of Lack of Ability: An Underexplored Aspect of Goal Theory." *Journal of Educational Psychology* 89, 710–18.

Mossholder, K. W. 1980. "Effects of Externally Mediated Goal Setting on Intrinsic Motivation: A Laboratory Experiment." *Journal of Applied Psychology* 65, 202–10.

Neveh-Benjamin, M., W. McKeachie, and Y. G. Lin. 1987. "Two Types of Test-Anxious Students: Support for an Information Processing Model." *Journal of Educational Psychology* 79, 131–36.

Newman, R. S. 1994. "Adaptive Help-Seeking: A Strategy of Self-Regulated Learning." In *Self-Regulation of Learning and Performance: Issues and Educational Applications*, ed. D. H. Schunk and B. J. Zimmerman, 283–301. Hillsdale, N.J.: Erlbaum.

Perreault, G. 2000. "The Classroom Impact of High-Stakes Testing." *Education* 120, no. 4, 705–10.

Pintrich, P. R., and E. V. de Groot. 1990. "Motivational and Self-Regulated Learning Components of Classroom Academic Performance." *Journal of Educational Psychology* 82, 32–40.

Pintrich, P. R., and D. H. Schunk. 2002. *Motivation in Education: Theory, Research, and Applications.* Upper Saddle River, N.J.: Merrill Prentice Hall.

Rawsthorne, L., and A. J. Elliot. 1999. "Achievement Goals and Intrinsic Motivation: A Meta-Analytic Review." *Personality and Social Psychology Review* 3, 326–44.

Reeve, J. 1996. *Motivating Others: Nurturing Inner Motivational Resources.* Boston: Allyn and Bacon.

Ryan, R. M. 1982. "Control and Information in the Intrapersonal Sphere: An Extension of Cognitive Evaluation Theory." *Journal of Personality and Social Psychology* 43, 450–61.

Ryan, R. M., and J. P. Connell. 1989. "Perceived Locus of Causality and Internalization: Examining Reasons for Acting in Two Domains." *Journal of Personality and Social Psychology* 57, 749–61.

Ryan, R. M., J. P. Connell, and R. W. Plant. 1990. "Emotions in Non-Directed Text Learning." *Learning and Individual Differences* 2, 1–17.

Ryan, R. M., and W. S. Grolnick. 1986. "Origins and Pawns in the Classroom: Self-report and Projective Assessment of Individual Differences in Children's Perceptions." *Journal of Personality and Social Psychology* 50, 550–58.

Ryan, R. M., V. Mims, and R. Koestner. 1983. "Relation of Reward Contingency and Interpersonal Context to Intrinsic Motivation: A Review and Test Using Cognitive Evaluation Theory." *Journal of Personality and Social Psychology* 45, 736–50.

Sexton, T., and B. Tuckman. 1991. "Self-Beliefs and Behavior: The Role of Self-Efficacy and Outcome Expectation over Time." *Personality and Individual Differences* 12, 725–36.

Shapira, Z. 1976. "Expectancy Determinants of Intrinsically Motivated Behavior." *Journal of Personality and Social Psychology* 34, 1235–44.

Skaalvik, E. 1997. "Self-Enhancing and Self-Defeating Ego Orientation: Relations with Task Avoidance Orientation, Achievement, Self-Perceptions, and Anxiety." *Journal of Educational Psychology* 89, 71–81.

Smith, W. E. 1974. *The Effects of Social and Monetary Rewards on Intrinsic Motivation.* Ph.D. dissertation, Cornell University, Ithaca, N.Y.

Stipek, D. 1998. *Motivation to Learn: From Theory to Practice.* Boston: Allyn and Bacon.

Swann, W. B., and R. S. Pittman. 1977. "Initiating Play Activity of Children: The Moderating Influence of Verbal Cues on Intrinsic Motivation." *Child Development* 48, 1128–32.

Tobias, S. 1986. "Anxiety and Cognitive Processing of Instruction." In *Self-Related Cognitions in Anxiety and Motivation*, ed. R. Schwarzer, 35–54. Hillsdale, N.J.: Lawrence Erlbaum.

Tobias, S. 1992. "The Impact of Test Anxiety Cognition in School Learning." In *Advances in Test Anxiety Research* (vol. 7), ed. K. A. Hagtvet and T. B. Johnsen, 18–31. Amsterdam: Swets and Zeitlinger.

Topman, R., W. Kleijn, H. van der Ploeg, and E. Masset. 1992. "Test Anxiety, Cognitions, Study Habits, and Academic Performance: A Prospective Study." In *Advances in Test Anxiety Research* (vol. 7), ed. K. Hagtvet and T. Johnsen, 239–59. Amsterdam: Swets and Zeitlinger.

Vallerand, R. J. 1991. "A Motivational Analysis of High School Dropout." Unpublished manuscript, University of Quebec at Montreal, Montreal, Canada.

Vallerand, R. J., and R. Bissonnette. 1992. "Intrinsic, Extrinsic, and Amotivational Styles as Predictors of Behavior: A Prospective Study." *Journal of Personality* 60, 599–620.

Vallerand, R. J., and F. Reid. 1984. "On the Causal Effects of Perceived Competence on Intrinsic Motivation: A Test of Cognitive Evaluation Theory." *Journal of Sport Psychology* 6, 94–102.

Wheelock, A., D. J. Bebell, and W. Haney. 2000. "What Can Student Drawings Tell Us about High-Stakes Testing in Massachusetts?" *Teachers College Record*, November 2. www.tcrecord.org/Content.asp?ContentID = 10634 (accessed 24 July 2002).

Wideen, M. F., T. O'Shea, I. Pye, and G. Ivany. 1997. "High-stakes Testing and the Teaching of Science." *Canadian Journal of Education* 22, no. 4, 428–44.

Wolters, C., S. Yu, and P. R. Pintrich. 1996. "The Relation between Goal Orientation and Students' Motivational Beliefs and Self-Regulated Learning." *Learning and Individual Differences* 8, 211–38.

Yarbrough, T. L. 1999. "Teacher Perceptions of the North Carolina ABC Program and the Relationship to Classroom Practice." Ph.D. dissertation, University of North Carolina at Chapel Hill.

Zatz, S., and L. Chassin. 1985. "Cognitions of Test-Anxious Children under Naturalistic Test-Taking Conditions." *Journal of Consulting and Clinical Psychology* 53, 393–401.

Zeidner, M. 1994. "Personal and Contextual Determinants of Coping and Anxiety in an Evaluative Situation: A Prospective Study." *Personality and Individual Differences* 16, 899–918.

Zimmerman, B. 1995. "Self-Efficacy and Educational Development." In *Self-Efficacy in Changing Societies*, ed. A. Bandura, 202–31. New York: Cambridge University Press.

Zimmerman, B., and A. Bandura. 1994. "Impact of Self-Regulatory Influences on Writing Course Attainment." *American Educational Research Journal* 31, 845–62.

Zuckerman, M., J. Porac, D. Lathin, R. Smith, and E. L. Deci. 1978. "On the Importance of Self-Determination for Intrinsically Motivated Behavior." *Personality and Social Psychology Bulletin* 4, 443–46.

Chapter Six

No Child Left Untested: The Impact on Special Populations

I used to think that special students [those with disabilities] should be tested. They just didn't seem to be held to the same high standard as other students. Now everything is equal alright [sic] . . . ALL students feel the unfair pressure of performing on the test.

(Sandra Smith, lead teacher, Middle Grades Alternative Program)

As a result of the Individuals with Disabilities Education Act (IDEA) in 1997, all individuals, regardless of ability or disability, must participate in accountability programs. This mandate was issued in an effort to ensure that all individuals are held to appropriately rigorous standards. In previous years, exemptions were issued to protect disadvantaged groups of students such as those with disabilities from any negative outcomes associated with standardized testing, such as grade level retention. Those in favor of exemptions generally support the use of alternative assessment for special populations. Those against exemptions feel that exemptions cause some students to be unfairly excluded from the educational program. Some opponents even claim that low-performing but capable students have been referred to special education programs in increased numbers for the purpose of being exempted from high-stakes tests. Eliminating this part of the student population increases the likelihood that low scorers will not pull down the school's rating. Clearly, both sides present plausible arguments.

Not only does federal law require that all students participate in standards-based accountability reform efforts, but it also mandates that testing programs publish disaggregated data on student performance (IDEA, 1997). Data must be disaggregated at the state, district, and school levels according to the following categories: economically disadvantaged, gender, ethnicity, migrant, limited English proficient, and disabled. The law also requires states to provide alternate assessments for severely disabled students who cannot participate in regular testing.

In response to the federal mandates of the Individuals with Disabilities Act and of No Child Left Behind, great emphasis has been placed on statewide testing as a means of determining academic achievement status. While many believe that this legislation is needed to ensure that all students are receiving a free and appropriate education, some teachers report that they do not feel that tests are fair for all students. Students with disabilities, students with limited English proficiency, those of low socioeconomic status, or those belonging to particular minority groups may be at risk of failure in a high-stakes testing environment.

"Failing the test" has taken on new meaning in many states as implementation of high-stakes accountability programs becomes the trend nationwide. As discussed previously, test scores are linked to important outcomes for schools, teachers, and students. Schools are rated according to how well their students score on the tests, and this rating has a bearing on many factors from retaining teachers to the value of real estate in the community. Teachers are often evaluated on the same criteria as the school, and in many states, test scores are tied to teacher bonuses. An inability to demonstrate mastery of the curriculum can also result in many undesirable outcomes for a student, including grade level retention. Many fear that mandated testing of all students will lead to disproportionate grade level retention for special needs students.

Grade level retention is a strong predictor of whether a student will drop out of school (Grissom and Shepard, 1989). As will be discussed further in chapter 7, research has demonstrated repeatedly that students who are retained have a greater chance of becoming high school dropouts. Students who are retained once are 20 to 30 percent more likely to drop out of school than their peers with equally poor achievement who are not retained, and students who have been retained twice have a probability of almost 100 percent of dropping out (Shepard and Smith, 1989). Even if these statistically vulnerable students escape retention and are able to stay in school through twelfth grade, they may yet have to pass a high school exit exam before graduation.

These high stakes have a tremendous impact on classroom policies and practices. Now that a larger percentage of a school's student body is tested, there are reports of some teachers encouraging low-performing students to miss school the day the test is administered. These teachers are concerned that their rankings will suffer if these students are allowed to take the test, and parents are told that taking the test would only result in a failure that would put the child further behind. Some states such as North Carolina have instituted policies that require a large percentage (virtually the entire school population) to be present for the test so that inflating school scores by encouraging low performers to stay at home is unlikely.

Many researchers believe that the high-stakes accountability movement will have the greatest impact on minorities, students with disabilities, students from low-status socioeconomic communities, and students with limited English proficiency. This chapter examines these groups to see how they have fared traditionally and how they are being affected by the testing movement. Alternatives and suggestions for meeting the needs of students belonging to special populations are discussed.

STUDENTS WITH DISABILITIES

Several reasons have been cited by the Office of Special Education Programs for advocating testing of special education students. The list includes improving educational results for children with disabilities, creating high educational expectations for all children, and holding schools accountable for educating all students (Office of Special Education and Rehabilitative Services and Office of Special Education Programs, 2000). No longer is it a matter of simply "meeting the needs" of special education students. As noted previously, the Individuals with Disabilities Education Act (IDEA) Amendments of 1997 call for the testing of all students.

According to the IDEA, students with disabilities must be provided equal access to educational programs, services, and activities. This includes equal access to earning a diploma and meeting eligibility requirements for honors programs and advanced placement classes, activities that are typically linked to performance on a standardized test (Disability Rights Advocates, 2001).

As of fall 2000, twenty-three states required students to pass a high school exit examination. As of the publication of this book, seven other states plan to implement exit exams within the coming three years. In addition to requiring that students pass a test to graduate, other states use standardized tests to make high-stakes decisions such as eligibility for advanced courses, honors classes, and scholarships. In 2001, approximately thirteen states used standardized tests to determine whether a student was promoted or retained in a grade (Disability Rights Advocates, 2001). This is particularly frightening given the fact that minorities and students with disabilities tend to fail at higher rates than other students, even on graduation tests that tend to focus on basic, minimal skills (Heubert, 2001).

Students with disabilities have, perhaps, even more to lose when it comes to standardized, high-stakes testing. Research suggests that when these students do not perform well on standardized tests, they are often given more remedial drill and practice of basic skills in an effort to increase their achievement. Students with disabilities are the ones that typically need high-quality programs the most, and in many cases, they are often the victims of poor instruction through low-level drill and are more likely to be subject to low expectations from teachers.

According to the IDEA, a student's individualized education plan (IEP) team is responsible for making decisions related to the child's participation in statewide and districtwide assessments. The IEP team is also responsible for determining what, if any, accommodations or modifications the child will receive. This means that students with disabilities who can benefit from accommodations and modifications must be provided with them.

The fact that students receive different accommodations raises a red flag among some test administrators interested in maintaining the technical quality (reliability and validity) of the test. Concern has been expressed about whether or not the use of accommodations places these students at an unfair advantage. To make the matter extremely complex, different questions arise depending on the type of disability or combination of disabilities and the specific accommodation. Students who are severely disabled must be given some form of alternate examination such as portfolio assessment, oral presentations, interviews, or projects. While such alternate assessments are an option for severely disabled students, some argue that these assessment results are difficult to compare to regular test results (Ysseldyke et. al, 1998).

As different states begin to administer high-stakes tests, some have implemented across-the-board policies that limit accommodations and modifications, even though federal law prohibits such policy. As a result, some states have had lawsuits filed against them because they failed to provide appropriate accommodations to special needs students. For example, on 21 February 2002, a federal judge ordered the California Board of Education to provide necessary accommodations (the use of calculators and other aids) to 45,000 high school students identified as having learning disabilities. This ruling also required that the state find alternative ways to assess students who could not pass the exam due to their disabilities.

The California exam, which includes both math and language arts, will be a requirement for graduation beginning in 2004. When the exam was given in the spring of 2001, 91 percent of the disabled students who took the test failed the math portion, compared to 52 percent of students who were not disabled. Eighty-two percent failed the language arts section, while 31 percent of nondisabled students failed this section of the exam. This failure took place despite accommodations such as spell-checkers and additional time. Originally, the California State Board of Education instituted policy that did not permit students to receive accommodations or modifications. In December of 2001, the Board modified its policy such that schools could use calculators and reading aids, if individual districts applied for and received a waiver (Wrightslaw Advocacy and Law Libraries, 2002).

The issues surrounding the assessment of special education students are particularly complex. For example, how can students be held accountable if they cannot express what they know? For some, it may be a situation in which testing modifications can be implemented to make this possible, but what happens to individuals who are not capable and are not likely to ever be capable of demonstrating mastery of such objectives? Consider the rare "idiot savant." The movie *Rain Man* provides a perfect example. While Raymond, the title character, was a mathematical genius able to count and calculate at speeds comparable to a computer, he couldn't even carry on a normal conversation. The Raymonds in our schools most certainly cannot demonstrate proficiency on standardized, multiple-choice reading tests. With legislation requiring that all students participate in statewide accountability programs and with a movement to end social promotion, what will schools do with exceptional students like Raymond?

As a result of recent legislation, the International Dyslexia Association, the National Center for Learning Disabilities, and the Learning Disabilities Association of America have published a list of thirteen core principles to ensure fair treatment of all students (International Dyslexia Association, 2001). A few of these principles endorsed by these societies are cited below:

1. Special needs students should be protected so that they have the same opportunity to participate in the curriculum and high-stakes tests. Likewise, tests should be free of bias and discrimination to afford all students an equal opportunity.
2. Special needs students should continue to receive all necessary accommodations and modifications in the classroom and on high-stakes tests as specified by the individual's individualized educa-

tion program or Section 504 plan. (Section 504 is a civil rights law that prohibits discrimination against individuals with disabilities. Section 504 ensures that disabled children have equal access to education.)

3. Students who cannot participate in high-stakes testing due to a specific disability must be assessed in some alternative way.
4. Alternative assessments should be available to all students who need them. It is inappropriate to designate a predetermined number or percentage of students who can participate in alternative assessments.

Progress is being made toward providing students with the accommodations and alternative assessments suggested by these principles. A recent survey of state directors of special education found that not only were more students with disabilities participating in accountability programs, but in addition, students with special needs had improved performance and were more likely to be offered testing accommodations (Thompson and Thurlow, 2001). Thompson and Thurlow (2001) also reported the following positive consequences for students with disabilities: accommodations allowed many students the option to pursue a regular high school diploma, more parents became aware of standards and assessments, there was increased use of assistive technology for students with disabilities, and there was greater involvement of special education personnel in staff development that addressed instruction toward standards. The researchers also found a number of negative consequences of participation of students with disabilities in assessment programs, including state assessments that were too difficult, students with disabilities causing schools to look less effective, more paperwork, students traumatized by taking tests, students with disabilities facing the possibility of not graduating, and students with disabilities remaining unable to reach the prescribed standard. These results show that high-stakes accountability programs provide students with disabilities with unique and difficult challenges and problems that must be weighed against the potential benefits of these testing programs.

ETHNIC GROUPS

Just as students with disabilities are disadvantaged when it comes to high-stakes testing, so are members of certain ethnic groups. Historically, minorities have not fared as well academically as their white counterparts. According to the Applied Research Center, "on nearly every key indicator—dropout rates, disciplinary rates, graduation rates, and college entrance rates, there are significant disparities across race in our schools" (Applied Research Center, 2000b, para. 5). Test data from the 1999 Massachusetts Comprehensive Assessment System indicate that minority students scored significantly lower than their white counterparts. In Boston, 85 percent of Hispanic tenth graders failed the test, while only 43 percent of white students failed. In fact, Hispanic students were the lowest scorers among all minority groups (Education World, 2000a). Other studies support this finding. In a 1999 study, Natriello and Pallas reported that substantial racial and ethnic disparities were evident on the Texas Assessment of Academic Skills (TAAS). They found that students in the white majority peer group consistently outscored African American and Hispanic students (Natriello and Pallas, 1999).

This gap in achievement continues to be a real stumbling block for minority students today, in spite of the fact that high-stakes tests have been touted for their ability to hold all students to a high standard. Many believe that the act of simply raising expectations for this population would help them to perform. On the contrary, minority students as a group continue to perform less well than their majority peers. It is important to note that simply being a member of a minority group does not mean that a student will be underperforming. There are students in all minority groups who excel in schools. But the issue is complicated by the fact that minorities have traditionally been given fewer resources and been denied equal educational opportunities in the educational system. In addition, many schools with low achievement scores serve large numbers of minorities from rural or urban areas that are poor.

The implications for underachieving minorities are numerous. Instead of improving conditions to reduce the achievement gap, the inequalities are even more pronounced, as students might receive more drill and practice in an effort to boost test scores. This kind of poor classroom preparation leads to long-term consequences including higher dropout rates. Historically, minorities have dropped out at significantly higher rates than whites. In 1999, the Hispanic dropout rate (28.6 percent) was four times as high as the dropout rates for whites (7.3 percent), and twice as many black students (12.6 percent) as whites dropped out of school in 1999 (National Center for Education Statistics, 2001).

Similarly, there are also great disparities across race when it comes to disciplinary actions. African American students, Latinos, and Native American students are suspended or expelled in greater numbers than their white counterparts. In 1999, the Applied Research Center launched a study of communities in several U.S. cities to see how schools fared on a number of indicators including student discipline. Every school district surveyed reported that minorities were disciplined more frequently than white students (Applied Research Center, 2000a). This finding is significant, as it impacts factors such as dropout rate. Studies show that an increased number of school suspensions is related to an increase in the number of students who drop out (Sinclair, 1997; Wehlage et al., 1989; Woods, 2001).

While many minority students still overcome the odds, they are once again at a disadvantage, as they are much less likely to complete a professional program of study once they leave high school. In 1995, only 6 percent of the Bachelor's degrees awarded in the physical sciences were earned by African Americans, even though they made up 12 percent of the U.S. population. Similarly, minorities are underrepresented in the scientific and technical workforce. In 1995, only 6 percent of the total science and engineering labor force was made up of African Americans, Hispanics, and Native Americans, yet these groups composed 23 percent of the total U.S. population (Green et al., 2000).

A close examination of the causes of the persistent achievement gap is needed. Despite the fact that the federal government is increasing spending to close the achievement gap, the gap continues to widen. Data from the 2001 Scholastic Aptitude Test (SAT) show a continued gap in achievement between minority students and their white peers, even though SAT averages rose for almost every racial ethnic group between 1991 and 2001. Average verbal scores for whites were up from 518 to 529 over the ten-year period. While improvements for African Americans were not as great (from 427 to 433), there still exists a ninety-six-point gap in achievement between white students and African Americans (Committee on Education and the Workforce, 2001).

Has the High-Stakes Testing Policy Helped Minorities?

To some, the attention given to school system and individual school test scores has drawn attention to schools that have been neglected for far too long. No longer can policy makers overlook schools that are failing to educate students. In North Carolina, schools in the most urban and rural settings that serve children from low socioeconomic groups often have the lowest scores. The public attention given to scores is also drawing attention to some schools that have historically underserved students. This is one of the positive benefits of the testing program. Schools can't hide from scores published in the newspaper, and when a school has low scores year after year, it is worth asking why. When a low socioeconomic status school that serves large numbers of minorities also makes high achievement scores, educators and the public can learn from the successes these schools make.

Researchers such as Lisa Delpit have recognized that for many minorities, test scores are the gatekeepers that may block students from colleges, scholarships, and careers that can provide a better life. "I have a kid now—brilliant. But he can't get a score on the SAT that will even get him considered by any halfway decent college" (Delpit, 1995, p. 16). In some cases, minority students have been allowed to flounder in majority classes. Testing programs highlight the achievement gap between minority and majority students and call attention to an underlying problem.

On the other hand, high-stakes testing programs may push schools and teachers to teach to the test in ways that emphasize the "basics" and de-emphasize critical thinking and problem solving skills. When this happens, minorities who are economically disadvantaged are hit doubly hard—not only do they tend to have lower scores on high-stakes tests that may block them from subsequent opportunities, but the instruction that they receive may actually be worse than the instruction that they received before the testing policy was implemented. These are often the students who lack access to libraries filled with books, come from homes where parents work two or more jobs, and live in areas without access to museums, aquaria, and symphonies. As we have discussed in this book, high-stakes testing policies often strip away the so-called "fluff" of education (art, music, foreign languages, and even science) to help children focus on the "basics" of mathematics, reading, and writing. The children who are losing access to a richer curriculum are often the ones who need it the most. Further research is needed to document how testing policies may be differentially impacting majority and minority children from different cultures, backgrounds, and socioeconomic groups.

ENGLISH LANGUAGE LEARNERS

In 1998, one out of three children in the United States was from an ethnic or racial minority group, one out of seven spoke a language other than English at home, and one out of fifteen was born outside the United States (Garcia, 1998). The increasing number of immigrants challenges United States schools to ensure that English Language Learners (ELLs), those for whom English is not their first language, are included in all aspects of schooling.

By the end of the 2000–2001 school year, each state was required to have an assessment system in place that included ELLs (Menken, 2000). The Improving America's Schools Act (IASA) states: "limited English proficient students . . . shall be assessed to the extent practical in the language and form most likely to yield accurate and reliable information on what students know and can do to determine such students' mastery of skills and subjects other than English"(United States Congress, 1994, sec. 1111). With new emphasis on including this segment of the population in large-scale testing, states must consider the fairness and accuracy of such tests for these special students.

Reasons for including this segment of the population in testing are parallel to those cited for including students with disabilities. It is believed that testing all students is the only way to ensure that this segment of the population also benefits from high standards. Rivera and Stansfield (1998) state: "inclusion in the testing program helps to remind districts and schools that students will need to receive at least the same quality and the same amount of content instruction as is given to other students" (p. 67). Problems arise, however, when states employ standardized tests that were not developed for the assessment of ELLs. According to the National Clearinghouse for Bilingual Education, most states employ tests that were developed to assess native English speakers (Menken, 2000).

Tests provide information about a student's knowledge that can be used to compare a student with other children of the same age. If a child's language and culture differ from those to which he or she is being compared, the conclusions drawn from the comparison may be inaccurate. For example, if a child does not understand English but is expected to complete a math word problem written in English, a low test score may be more indicative of the child's ability to understand English than the particular math skill being assessed. From this score alone, one might incorrectly conclude that the child is deficit in the area of mathematics, whereas the student may actually be gifted in mathematics.

Research tells us that language proficiency is strongly linked to performance on standardized tests. Students identified as ELLs score significantly lower than non-ELL students on many science and math questions (Abedi and Leon, 1999). Interestingly enough, the gap in performance decreases significantly (to the point that it almost disappears) on math items that require no specific language skills, such as math computation (Abedi, Leon, and Mirocha, 2001).

Like other groups at risk of failing standardized tests, students who speak limited English have been shown to be at greater risk of dropping out of high school. In 1995, students who reported that they did not speak English well had a 32.9 percent dropout rate, compared to a 19.2 percent dropout rate for those who reported speaking English well or very well (McMillen, Kaufman, and Klein, 1997).

The National Center for Research on Evaluation, Standards, and Student Testing (CRESST) makes a number of recommendations to policy makers and educators based on their research related to ELL students (Abedi, 2001). The following are among those actions suggested:

1. Translate test items to the student's primary language of instruction, not their primary spoken language. For example, test items translated from English to other languages may not prove to be helpful if ELL students are taught in English.
2. Ensure that test items are worded simply so as to reduce unnecessary complex language.
3. Provide testing accommodations to give ELL students the *same* opportunities as regular education students. ELL students should not be at an unfair disadvantage or advantage over other students. Simply put, accommodations should serve to provide access to the test; access that would not otherwise be gained due to the student's disability. For example, EEL students can benefit from customized dictionaries instead of providing an entire traditional dictionary.
4. Monitor and evaluate all intended and unintended effects of accommodations on EEL students and native English-speaking students. Accommodations should not impact native English-speaking students but should help to reduce the language barrier for ELL students.

LOW SOCIOECONOMIC STATUS

Traditionally, students in areas of low socioeconomic status have not done well on standardized tests. During the 1999–2000 school year, Louisiana test data revealed that large, urban school districts scored significantly lower than their smaller, suburban counterparts. For example, 63 percent of the eighth graders from the Orleans school district, an urban district, failed the math test compared to only 10 percent from the St. Tammany school district, a suburban district (Education World, 2000b).

The American Civil Liberties Union (ACLU) of Massachusetts issued a public advisory expressing concern that the Massachusetts Comprehensive Assessment System (MCAS) discriminated against particular socioeconomic and ethnic groups. According to the ACLU:

> between 80 and 90 percent of African American and Latino students across the state [of Massachusetts] will not receive their high school diplomas. The testing gap between rich and poor communities remains as wide as ever, with 65 percent of students in low income districts but only 12 percent of students in affluent towns failing a portion of the test. Although the graduation requirement does not become effective until 2003, already there is evidence that students are discouraged and are dropping out, are not being promoted, and possibly are encouraged to drop out so as not to affect a town's MCAS average. (ACLU of Massachusetts, 2000)

A study by the Alberta Teachers' Association, Edmonton Public Schools, and Department of Education Student Evaluation Branch found that socioeconomic status accounted for about half of the variance in the Edmonton Public Schools' test scores. In fact, socioeconomic status was by far the single most important factor accounting for the variance in student test scores (Alberta Teachers' Association, 1997).

We have known for years that socioeconomic status is the greatest predictor of academic achievement. Students who come from wealthier backgrounds have usually been exposed to much richer experiences, experiences that equate to success on standardized tests. Children who have been read to, been exposed to printed materials and pictures, have visited museums, and have watched educational television are certainly more likely to identify with the scenarios presented on standardized tests.

Socioeconomic characteristics such as parent's occupation or level of income are so heavily correlated to success on standardized tests that some claim that a child's tests scores can be determined by a factor known as the Volvo effect: Simply count the number of Volvos, BMWs, or Mercedes owned by the family and you have a good indicator of how well the child will perform on standardized tests. Some researchers advance the Volvo measure as a good way to save millions of dollars on standardized tests. Jonathon Kozol argues: "(p)oliticians who advocate tougher standards and high-stakes testing of children without providing equal resources to help all children succeed are practicing 'punitive hypocrisy'" (Wisconsin Education Association Council, 2000).

Unfortunately, some students belong to more than one of the groups being described in this chapter. For example, Hispanic students, in addition to being in a minority group, may belong to a lower socioeconomic group. About 40 percent of Hispanic children live in poverty, as compared to 15 percent of their white peers (Rumberger, 1991). Additionally, testing does little to change the underlying conditions of poverty, language, access, or culture that contribute to the lower scores of underachieving groups. Just as Representative Bill Goodling has noted, "you cannot fatten cattle by weighing them" (Neill, 1998, p. 45), and you can't improve school quality if all you do is test.

Alternatives and Suggestions for Improvement

There are a number of strategies that educators and policy makers can implement to reduce the factors that place groups of students at risk for test failure. These include the following:

1. Allow students who are not proficient to get extra help after school or during the summer.

Some children simply require more time to learn. It is quite reasonable that students who do not speak English, who have a learning disability, or who have a physical disability may need more time to master concepts and skills. The school should implement programs that allow students who need additional help to receive it either before or after school, on Saturday, or during the summer.

Students should advance to the next grade level prepared for the next curriculum. Retaining students in-grade should not be the method for remediating students who have fallen behind. Instead, students should be offered interventions that are early and intensive.

2. Allow special testing accommodations for special needs students.

Students with special needs should be allowed appropriate accommodations so that they may demonstrate the knowledge and skills measured by standardized tests. Accommodations should include, but not be limited to, extended time, quiet rooms, customized dictionaries or glossaries for English Language Learners, scribes or readers, the use of computers or word processors, spell checkers, dictation machines, audio test materials, and/or adaptive equipment. Accommodations should be provided so all students can be evaluated by the same standards.

3. Recruit, employ, and retain competent faculty members who reflect the diversity of the student population.

It is important that a school faculty have a similar racial makeup as the student population. Minority students need to see adults with similar racial backgrounds as teachers and school leaders. Schools should establish school cultures and climates that are inclusive of all students regardless of background, culture, or socioeconomic status. School districts should encourage minorities to choose teaching as a career. Minority students should also be encouraged to take advanced mathematics and science courses.

4. Provide meaningful professional development opportunities to enable teachers and administrators to work effectively with diverse learners.

Teachers and administrators should be given ample opportunities to participate in meaningful professional development designed to help them reach a wide variety of learners. When individualized instruction is used, it should be data-driven, informed by student performance data (Missouri Department of Elementary and Secondary Education, 1997).

5. Invite successful minority adults to serve as role models for young minority students.

Successful minority adults should be invited into the school on a regular basis to visit with classes and individual students about their positions. All too often, athletes and entertainers are used as role models for young minority students, and students may fail to see themselves as future scientists, mathematicians, or engineers. It is critical that these minority students also see adults from a wide range of careers (Missouri Department of Elementary and Secondary Education, 1997).

6. Provide data from statewide testing programs that can be used to inform planning and instruction.

Data provided from statewide standardized tests should provide specific and detailed information about the skills and concepts that individual students have mastered and still need to master. This information can be used for planning professional development opportunities as well as remedial programs, such as summer school and after-school programs. Such information would also be useful to districts when ensuring that the assessments are aligned with the curriculum.

7. Embrace the notion that learning must be demonstrated through tasks that are real and not just measured by regurgitating facts.

Performance-based assessment incorporates the use of authentic demonstrations of students' abilities. Even if standardized tests are required at the state or district level, educators should seek more appropriate and valid methods of assessment for informing their instruction and determining what a student knows and can do. For many students with language disabilities, or those who may not read and write English as their first language, the use of performance assessments allows them to show what they know irrespective of their use of language.

8. Align assessments with the curriculum and classroom instruction.

If special populations are going to be successful with the implementation of standards-based reform, tests must match what is taught in the classroom. If tests are constructed carefully, this notion can become a powerful opportunity to inform classroom practice.

9. Always use multiple methods of assessment when making high-stakes decisions.

Advice from the National Research Council (1999) of the National Academy of Sciences is echoed by professional organizations and institutions. The Council states, "An educational decision that will have a major impact on a test taker should not solely or automatically be made on the basis of a single test score. Other relevant information about the student's knowledge and skills should also be taken into account" (National Research Council, 1999, pp. 275–76). It adds: "High-stakes decisions such as tracking, promotion, and graduation should not automatically be made on the basis of a test score but should be buttressed by other relevant information about the student's knowledge and skills" (p. 279). Factors such as grades, effort, and demonstrated improvement should be considered when making important decisions.

REFERENCES

Abedi, J. 2001. "Assessment and Accommodations for English Language Learners: Issues and Recommendations." *Policy Brief 4, National Center for Research on Evaluation, Standards, and Student Learning (CRESST).* Los Angeles: Author. www.cse.ucla.edu/CRESST/Newsletters/Polbrf4web.pdf (accessed 15 July 2002).

Abedi, J., and S. Leon. 1999. *Impact of Students' Language Background on Content-Based Performance: Analyses of Extant Data.* Los Angeles: University of California, National Center for Research on Evaluation, Standards, and Student Testing.

Abedi, J., S. Leon, and J. Mirocha. 2001. *Impact of Students' Language Background on Standardized Achievement Test Results: Analyses of Extant Data.* Los Angeles: University of California, National Center for Research on Evaluation, Standards, and Student Testing.

Alberta Teachers' Association. 1997. "Socio-Economic Status Strong Predictor of Performance." Volume 33, no. 2. Publication of the Alberta Teacher's Association.

American Civil Liberties Union of Massachusetts. 2000. Public Advisory. www.aclu
-mass.org/youth/studentrights/mcasadvisory.html (accessed 15 July 2002).

American Federation of Teachers. 1999. *Making Standards Matter 1999*. Washington, D.C.: Author.

Applied Research Center. 2000a. "Facing the Consequences: An Examination of Racial Discrimination in the U.S. Public Schools." www.arc.org/ERASE/FTC1intro.html (accessed 15 July 2002).

Applied Research Center. 2000b. "Get Smart: Standards for Excellence and Equity in Public Education." www.arc.org/erase/smart.html (accessed 15 July 2002).

Committee on Education and the Workforce. 2001. Press release. edworkforce .house.gov/press/press107/sat82801.htm (accessed 15 July 2002).

Delpit, L. 1995. *Other People's Children*. New York: The New Press.

Disability Rights Advocates. 2001. "Do No Harm: High Stakes Testing and Students with Learning Disabilities." www.dralegal.org/publications/dnh.pdf (accessed 15 July 2002).

Education World. 2000a. "Are High Stakes Punishing Some Students?" www .education-world.com/a_issues/issues093.shtml (accessed 15 July 2002).

Education World. 2000b. "Should Standardized Tests Determine Who Is Held Back?" http://www.education-world.com/a_issues/issues089.shtml (accessed 24 November 2002).

Garcia, E. 1998. *Excellence and Equity for Language Minority Students: Critical Issues and Promising Practices*. Chevy Chase, Md.: The Mid-Atlantic Equity Center.

Green, L. R., K. Blasik, K. Hartshorn, and E. Schatten-Jones. 2000. "Closing the Achievement Gap in Science: A Program to Encourage Minority and Female Students to Participate and Succeed." *ERS Spectrum*, Spring. www.ers.org/spectrum/ spg00a.htm (accessed 15 July 2002).

Grissom, K. B., and L. A. Shepard. 1989. "Repeating and Dropping out of School." In *Flunking Grades: Research and Policies on Retention*, ed. L. A. Shepard and M. L. Smith, 34–63. Philadelphia, Pa.: Falmer Press.

Heubert, J. P. 2001. "High-Stakes Testing: Opportunities and Risks for Students of Color, English-Language Learners, and Students with Disabilities." www.cast .org/ncac/index.cfm?I-920 (accessed 15 July 2002).

Improving America's Schools Act. 1994. Public Law 103–227. 103rd Cong., 2nd sess., 25 January.

Individuals with Disabilities Education Act. 1997. Public Law 105–17. 105th Cong., 2nd sess., 7 January. 20 U.S.C., Ch. 33, §§ 1400–1491.

International Dyslexia Association. 2001. "Thirteen Core Principles to Ensure Fair Treatment of All Students, Including Those with Learning Disabilities, with Regard to High Stakes Assessments." www.interdys.org/servlet/compose?section_ id=1andpage_id=146 (accessed 15 August 2002).

McMillen, M., P. Kaufman, and S. Klein. 1997. *Dropout Rates in the United States: 1995*. Washington, D.C.: United States Department of Education, National Center for Educational Statistics, 97–473. Issue Brief no. 6, pp. 1–6.

Menken, K. 2000. "What Are the Critical Issues in Wide-Scale Assessment of

English Language Learners?" National Clearinghouse for Bilingual Education Center for the Study of Language and Education website. www.ncbe.gwu.edu/ncbepubs/tasynthesis/framing/3criticalissues.htm (accessed 15 August 2002).

Missouri Department of Elementary and Secondary Education. 1997. "Raising the Bar—Closing the Gap: Recommendations for Improving the Academic Achievement of African-American Students in Missouri." www.dese.state.mo.us/news/academicreport.htm (accessed 15 August 2002).

National Center for Education Statistics. 2001. *The Condition of Education 2001, NCES 2001–072.* Washington, D.C.: U.S. Government Printing Office.

National Research Council. 1999. *High Stakes: Testing for Tracking, Promotion, and Graduation*, ed. J. Heubert and R. Hauser. Washington, D.C.: National Academy Press.

Natriello, G., and A. Pallas. 1999. "The Development and Impact of High Stakes Testing." Cambridge, Mass.: Civil Rights Project, Harvard University.

Neill, M. 1998. "National Tests are Unnecessary and Harmful." *Educational Leadership 55*, no. 6, 45–46.

Office of Special Education and Rehabilitative Services and Office of Special Education Programs. 2000. "Assessment Report 00–24." www.wrightslaw.com/law/reports/osep_memorandum_assessment_000824.pdf (accessed 15 August 2002).

Rivera, C., and C. Stansfield. 1998. "Leveling the Playing Field for English Language Learners: Increasing Participation in State and Local Assessments through Accommodations." In *Assessing Student Learning: New Rules, New Realities*, ed. R. Brandt, 65–92. Arlington, Va: Educational Research Service.

Rumberger, R. 1991. "Chicano Dropouts: A Review of Research and Policy Issues." In *Chicano School Failure and Success*, ed. R. Valencia, 64–89. New York: Falmer Press.

Shepard, L. S., and M. L. Smith. 1989. *Flunking Grades: Research and Policies on Retention.* London: Falmer.

Sinclair, M. F. 1997. *Dropout Prevention Issues Concerning Youth with and without Disabilities.* Transcript of NTA Conference Call Presentation held on 18 March 1997. ici2.coled.umn.edu/ntn/audio/1997/mar.html (accessed 15 August 2002).

Thompson, S., and M. Thurlow. 2001. *State Special Education Outcomes: A Report on State Activities at the Beginning of a New Decade.* Minneapolis, Minn.: University of Minnesota, National Center on Educational Outcomes. education.umn.edu/NCEO/OnlinePubs/2001StateReport.html (accessed 3 September 2002).

Wehlage, G., R. Rutter, G. Smith, N. Lesko, and R. Fernandez. 1989. *Reducing the Risk: Schools as Communities of Support.* Philadelphia, Pa.: Falmer.

Wisconsin Education Association Council. 2000. "Kozol Sees Hypocrisy in Testing Craze." Keynote address given to the Wisconsin Education Association Council Convention, Madison, Wisc., 25–27 October.

Woods, E. G. 2001. "Reducing the Dropout Rate: Close-Up #17." School Improvement Series, Northwest Regional Educational Laboratory website. www.nwrel.org/scpd/sirs/9/c017.html (accessed 15 August 2002).

Wrightslaw Advocacy and Law Libraries. 2002. "Judge Orders California to Provide LD Students with Accommodations on High School Exit Exam." www.wrightslaw.com/news/2002/ca.injunction.accoms.htm (accessed 15 August 2002).

Ysseldyke, J. E., M. L. Thurlow, E. Kozleski, and D. Reschly. 1998. "Accountability for the Results of Educating Students with Disabilities: Assessment Conference Report on the New Assessment Provisions of the 1997 Amendments to the Individuals with Disabilities Education Act." Minneapolis, Minn.: University of Minnesota, National Center on Educational Outcomes. education.umn.edu/NCEO/ OnlinePubs/awgfinal.html (accessed 15 August 2002).

Chapter Seven

Missing the Mark:
Testing and Student Retention

During the last week of school, Latika Jones clutched her fourth grade teacher in her arms. As her teacher asked, "Now what will you do next year without me?" Latika responded, "I thought I'd just stay here in fourth grade with you!" Latika didn't know her words would become reality.

For the past two years, Latika had responded very well to Mrs. Weaver. Mrs. Weaver had been fortunate enough to keep her students for a second year; after third grade was finished, Mrs. Weaver had moved with the class to fourth grade. This consistency benefited Latika tremendously. After all, Mrs. Weaver was aware of what Latika knew and could do, so months of preliminary assessment were eliminated. Mrs. Weaver could get "right down to business" with this child who needed her help so desperately. But even with saving so much time at the beginning of the year, Mrs. Weaver felt that her efforts were not enough. She began to tutor Latika after school in reading. Latika's grades had improved from the previous year, and she had made all Bs and Cs, demonstrating that she could compete with other fourth grade students. Mrs. Weaver just knew that all this hard work would pay off when Latika took her end-of-grade test in May.

When scores were returned, Mrs. Weaver nervously scanned her list looking for Latika's name. Math was first, and boy, did she knock the top off! Latika made a 4, the highest score given on the end-of-grade test! Next was reading . . . Mrs. Weaver took a deep breath and hoped for at least a passing score! As she looked down her list, she found the name . . . Latika Jones . . . 2. Latika had failed the end-of-grade test! All that work for a 2! How could this be? How close was Latika to earning a 3? By scanning the list of developmental scale scores, Mrs. Weaver found a child on her list just three points higher than Latika with a 3 by his name! She had come so far to have "failure" stamped by her name, and she was so close! Mrs. Weaver knew that in fifth grade, a 2 would never suffice with the implementation of the new North Carolina gateways, which state that all fifth graders must score level 3 in reading and math in order to be promoted to sixth grade. Mrs. Weaver also knew that Latika was a much better reader than was reflected by this score.

A disappointed Mrs. Weaver walked to the office to check her mailbox before leaving for the day. As she pulled the cold, white sheet of school letterhead from her box, she read that in order to prepare students for gateway years (third and fifth grade), fourth graders were also being held to the same high standards. Any student who did not score a level 3 in reading and math must be retained. Period. No discussion of how hard they had worked or the fact that some, like Latika, had already been retained once before! Never mind that in "gateway" years mandated by the state, students were given a second opportunity to take the test, and, if they did not make a 3, they were sent to summer school with a second retest given at the conclusion of summer school. No, Latika would have none of these opportunities. How could the system be so unfair? How would Mrs. Weaver explain this to Latika?

In April of 1999, the North Carolina State Board of Education passed its new Student Accountability Standards. The policy required students in third, fifth, and eighth grade to pass tests in reading, writing, and math in order to be promoted. Passing scores were defined as a 3 in reading and math and a score of 2.5 on the state's writing test. These new Student Accountability Standards, or "gateways," became effective during the 2000–2001 school year for fifth graders and during the 2001–2002 school year for third and eighth graders. The policy also states that high school students must pass an exam on computer and other essential skills. The intent of this component of the testing program is to end social promotion, the practice of moving students who have failed to master part or all of the grade-level curriculum on to the next grade with their same-age peers.

North Carolina is not alone. In his 1998 State of the Union Address, President Clinton vowed to improve schools by ending social promotion. As a result, many states are implementing retention policies for students who do not master part of all or the curriculum. These retention policies are generally tied to the high-stakes tests such that if students don't pass the tests, then they don't move on to the next grade level.

In this chapter, we examine the research on retention and argue that the practice of retaining students is in direct conflict with the research. It is difficult to understand how there can be so much support for retention when the research overwhelmingly shows the negative effects of this educational practice. Roy Doyle (1989) states: "There is probably no widespread practice in education today that has been as thoroughly discredited by research" (p. 215).

While retention is certainly not the cure-all, social promotion also has its shortcomings. Most agree that our schools should hold students to rigorous standards and that students should be required to master important material. Therefore, we also present alternatives to both retention and social promotion.

For the past thirty years, the pendulum has been swinging back and forth from social promotion to grade retention. It seems that with each decade, the pendulum swings in the opposite direction. Policy makers promote the use of retention in one decade only to oppose it in the next. During the 1970s, social promotion was the option of choice in light of the growing evidence about the negative effects of retention on students' self-esteem (Westchester Institute for Human Services Research, 2001). During the 1980s, concerns about students who were not prepared for college or the workplace facilitated the introduction of minimal competence testing and caused the pendulum to swing back in the direction of retention. By 1990, however, several large-city school districts including Boston, Chicago, New York, and Philadelphia were advocating that students be promoted with their same-age peers, as a result of research suggesting that grade retention contributed to increased dropout rates (McCollum et al., 1999; Westchester Institute for Human Services Research, 2001).

Now the pendulum has swung the other way. The North Carolina gateways sound all too familiar. Ernest House (1989) laments about 1981, when the New York City schools implemented a program called Promotional Gates. Much like the North Carolina Gateways program, this program was implemented so that students would be checked at designated "gates" or grade levels and those who had not mastered skills measured by state standardized tests would not be allowed to proceed. This program was designed to send a message to students and teachers that social promotion was no longer acceptable in New York City. During this year, the New York City schools retained 25,000 students in the fourth and seventh grades because of low test scores. The school system came to the conclusion that neither the students nor the teachers were trying hard enough and that both groups needed to be pressured into making the grade. Any fourth grade student who was more than one grade level behind on the district reading test, or any seventh grade student who was more than one and a half years behind, would be held back. This included approximately one-quarter of the students at those grade levels. The school system placed the retained students into special classes of twenty or fewer students with special teachers, materials, and programs. Students were expected to stay in these remedial classes until they demonstrated that their skills were up to par by performing on grade level on the next standardized test. During the first year alone, this program required about 1,100 additional teachers and cost the New York City schools more than 40 million dollars. The following year, the program was expanded to include mathematics achievement, and plans were made to expand to other subject areas in subsequent years.

Ernest House and two colleagues, Robert Linn and James Raths, all of the University of Illinois, were commissioned to evaluate the Promotional Gates program. For two years, they collected data, and when the data were compiled, they found that there were no substantial achievement differences between the students who had been held back and those in previous years who had been promoted. The evaluation was conducted again the next year, and the results were the same. The program was abandoned because it did not improve student academic achievement (House, 1989).

As students, particularly minorities and those from low-wealth districts, continue to perform poorly on achievement tests, many states are reinstating retention. In 1997, the Chicago Public Schools were ahead of the pendulum in ending social promotion. Students who did not master the curriculum at certain promotional gates were required to attend summer school to master the material or repeat the grade the following year (McCollum et al., 1999). In spite of the previous experience in the New York City School System, the present New York School Chancellor has called for an end to social promotion and has just reinstated the Promotional Gates program (Advocates for Children of New York, 2000). North Carolina followed their lead and retained students who did not pass the high-stakes tests.

THE RESEARCH ON RETENTION

The research on the negative effects of retention is very clear. Studies have demonstrated over and over that retention is harmful to students both academically and socially (Foster, 1993; Holmes and Mathews, 1984; Shepard and Smith, 1989; Walters and Borgers, 1995). According to McCollum et al. (1999), out of sixty-six studies conducted on retention from 1990 to 1997, sixty-five found it to be ineffective and/or harmful to students. There are many reasons cited in the literature for retention being an ineffective solution to underachievement.

No Academic Benefits

Research on retention shows that students who are retained do no better the second time in the same grade, and many actually do worse. McCollum et al. (1999) found that 50 percent of retained students did not perform better the second time, and 25 percent did worse. According to a meta-analysis conducted by Holmes (1989) which reviewed sixty-three controlled studies on how students perform after being retained, fifty-four studies showed that when children progressed to the next grade level after being retained, they performed more poorly on average than their same-age peers who were not retained. Linda Darling-Hammond (1998) maintains, "Students who are held back actually do worse in the long run than comparable students who are promoted, in part because they do not receive better or more appropriate teaching when they are retained, and in part because they give up on themselves as learners" (para. 4).

Only nine of the sixty-three studies that Holmes (1989) reviewed showed positive results, and most of these studies compared subjects who had received extra help through individualized programs. Additionally, all of these studies focused on suburban schools where most of the students, even before they were held back, did not have severe academic deficiencies. Although they did not score well enough to progress to the next grade level at their school, their test scores showed them to be of average IQ. Even in spite of the gains cited by Holmes in these nine studies, the increased benefits of retention tended to diminish over time so that there was no difference in students who had been retained and those who had not been retained.

Higher Dropout Rate

Retention is strongly linked to dropping out of school in later years (Grissom and Shepard, 1989). In the widely cited Youth in Transition study, researchers found that one grade retention increases the risk of dropping out by 40 percent to 50 percent. Two grade retentions increase the risk to 90 percent, almost guaranteeing that the student will not graduate from high school (Bachman, Green, and Wirtanen, 1971).

In North Carolina, an increasing number of high school students are not graduating. Since 1990, North Carolina's four-year graduation rate has dropped from about 66 percent to less than 56 percent. Almost half of all students are not graduating from North Carolina's schools on time. While this drop in graduation rate reflects a similar trend nationwide, it is more pronounced in North Carolina than in any other state except New Mexico, South Carolina, and Georgia ("Flip Side of Higher Standards," 2001). North Carolina education leaders strive to explain why the graduation rate is so low. One explanation is that the state's higher standards and promotion requirements might cause some students to spend additional time repeating grade levels or dropping out of school altogether.

Low Self-Esteem

Grade retention sends a clear message to students that they are not as competent as students who are not retained. The long-term negative effects on students' beliefs about their abilities as learners may outweigh any effect the remediation may have had on increased academic achievement.

Other studies demonstrate that students who are retained suffer lower self-esteem and view retention as a punishment and not as a positive outcome designed to help them achieve their academic goals (Byrnes, 1989; Holmes, 1989). Byrnes (1989) interviewed children using euphemisms to refer to spending two years in the same grade. Even first graders referred to repeating a grade by stating, "Oh, you mean flunking." An overwhelming 87 percent of the children interviewed said that being retained had negative consequences such as making them feel "sad," "upset," or "embarrassed." Only 6 percent of the students interviewed perceived retention in a positive way, stating positive outcomes of retention such as "you learn more." In an earlier study, Yamamoto (1980) asked children to rate repeating a grade against several life events. Students indicated that repeating a grade was more stressful than "wetting in class." The only two life events that children said would be more stressful than being retained were going blind or losing a parent.

Grade retention may increase the likelihood that a student will drop out because it causes the student to be older than other students in his or her class during adolescent years. For some students, this results in even greater feelings of frustration and disengagement.

Another reason for avoiding grade level retention is the notion that retention targets a select portion of the population. Retention rates are much higher for boys and members of minority groups (Hauser, 1999). Forty percent of students retained come from the lowest socioeconomic quartile, whereas their more privileged counterparts only make up 8.5 percent of the retained population (Meisels and Liaw, 1993).

High Cost

Retention is expensive. Retention costs the country an average of 10 billion dollars annually (McCollum et al., 1999). In 1995, Texas spent an average cost of $4,504 per retained student, but summer school only cost a fraction of this amount (Texas Education Agency, 2001). The money spent annually on retaining students would go a long way in providing alternatives to retention, such as remedial programs, reduced class size, classroom assistants, or summer school programs.

Even though there are general published statistics on retention expenses, the actual cost per student is not particularly clear. For example, if a student moves during his or her years of school, a student spending four years in a district will incur the same costs regardless of the grade levels in which he or she enrolls. By the time the student has reached the fourteenth or fifteenth year of school, it is unlikely that the student will live in the same district in which he or she was retained. It is possible, therefore, for many districts or states to bear the expense of retention for the same student (Shepard and Smith, 1990).

Developmental Differences

Given the naturally wide variation in development for children at any given age, it doesn't make much sense to place students into groups that move in lock step and advance at the end of a one-year period (Romey, 2000). Jim Grant, a former teacher, argues, "When you have 365 birth dates and two genders and kids who are low birth weight and are living in poverty, someone is going to be assigned to the wrong grade" (Kelly, 1999, para. 9).

Romey (2000) also states, " 'Retaining' a child who hasn't passed a certain level at the end of June isn't really 'retention' at all. It's moving the child clear back to the beginning of the year he or she has 'failed' rather than working with the individual child at his or her actual level of achievement" (Romey, 2000, p. 632).

As shown in this chapter, there is ample evidence that retention simply does not work. As a public, we Americans must question the efficacy of programs that employ retention tactics in an effort to meet the needs of all students. If we promote students to the next level without the necessary skills and we don't retain them until mastery is accomplished, what are the alternatives? How can we best meet the needs of all students?

ALTERNATIVES TO RETENTION AND SOCIAL PROMOTION

Unfortunately, retention is often seen as the only alternative to social promotion. A 1997 study by the American Federation of Teachers notes that neither retention nor social promotion is an adequate response to low student achievement, in large measure because neither approach requires a change in pedagogy, content, or curriculum. Retention also typically fails to address the serious family and learning problems that low-achieving students may have. The National Research Council (NRC) of the National Academy of Sciences agrees: "Neither social promotion nor retention alone is an effective treatment" (National Research Council, 1998, p. 278). The NRC report continues, "grade retention policies typically have positive intentions but negative consequences" (p. 285).

When alternatives are considered, they tend to be options such as placing students in remedial tracks that often become permanent. Options such as these operate on a "student deficit model." It is assumed that the student has control over his or her progress and ignores the possibility that the educational program may have played a part in the child's lack of success (McCollum et al., 1999). Neither retention nor social promotion is a satisfactory answer to the need for all students to compete in a rigorous curriculum. Research by Darling-Hammond (1998) supports the need to develop alternatives to both social promotion and retention. Alternatives suggested by Darling-Hammond (1998) and others include the following:

1. Redesign the structure of schools to support differences in developmental readiness. For instance, one solution would be to implement multiage classes in which teachers remain with the same students for more than one year.
2. Identify, as early as possible, students who are not achieving at grade level.

3. Provide services and programs to students who have not met grade level criteria. These might include tutoring, after-school programs, or Saturday classes.
4. As part of the student evaluation process, use classroom assessments that inform teaching and learning, such as anecdotal records, checklists, and rubrics.
5. Provide additional professional development opportunities for teachers in order to ensure that they have the knowledge and skills necessary to work with students who are at risk of failing.
6. If retention is used, establish limits on the number of times a student can be retained.
7. If retention is used, do not make retention decisions on the basis of one test score.

This last recommendation is of particular importance. Retention decisions should be made on multiple criteria rather than solely on high-stakes test scores or teacher recommendations. In 1999, the inappropriate reliance on a single test score was troublesome for the New York City schools when it was discovered that the standardized test was not normed properly and that thousands of students who failed should have passed (Archibold, 1999; Hartocollis, 1999).

On the contrary, just the opposite occurred in North Carolina. State school officials claimed that the end-of-grade math tests administered during the 2000–2001 school year were normed too low. In other words, some students who passed should have failed. The state had incorporated field questions onto the previous year's tests, but many students did not do well, so the state lowered its minimum score for passing. The state also believed that teachers helped to prepare students for the new tests, resulting in a higher passing rate ("State Officials Say Math Tests Too Easy," 2001). This problem raises some important concerns. How many tests have been administered on which the score designated as failing was not accurate and the public was not made aware? What constitutes the "right" score for failing? If teachers and students work extra hard to prepare for tests, shouldn't the result be a high passing rate?

Supporters of retention assume that students are being held to rigorous standards. As we have described in this chapter and other chapters in this book, the high-stakes tests may not measure the types of complex learning for which American schools are striving. While it is important that students experience a challenging curriculum, educators and policy makers must be aware of the research on retention that delineates so many negative consequences. If students were not successful the first time around, repeating an entire year of the same work will likely not produce success. It is time to look for more viable and appropriate means for challenging our nation's students.

REFERENCES

Advocates for Children of New York. 2000. "An Overview of National Research on the Effectiveness of Retention of Student Achievement." www.advocatesforchildren .org/pubs/retention.html (accessed 13 July 2002).

American Federation of Teachers. 1997. *Passing On Failure: District Promotion Policies and Practices*. Washington, D.C.: American Federation of Teachers. ERIC, ED 421 560.

Archibold, R. 1999. "8600 in Summer School by Error, Board Says." *New York Times*, 16 September.

Bachman, J. G., S. Green, and I. D. Wirtanen. 1971. *Dropping Out: Problem or Symptom?* Youth in Transition, vol. 3. Ann Arbor, Mich.: Institute for Social Research, University of Michigan.

Byrnes, D. A. 1989. "Attitudes of Students and Educators toward Repeating a Grade." In *Flunking Grades: Research and Policies on Retention*, ed. L. A. Shepard and M. L. Smith, 108–31. Philadelphia, Pa.: Falmer Press.

Darling-Hammond, L. 1998. "Alternatives to Grade Retention." *The School Administrator Web Edition*. www.aasa.org/publications/sa/1998_08/Darling-Hammond.htm (accessed 10 February 2003).

Doyle, R. 1989. "The Resistance of Conventional Wisdom to Research Evidence: The Case of Retention in Grade." *Phi Delta Kappan* 71, no. 3, 215–20.

"Flip Side of Higher Standards: A Rising Rate of Dropouts." 2001. *Raleigh News and Observer*, 1 April.

Foster, J. 1993. "Review of Research: Retaining Children in Grade." *Childhood Education* 70, 38–43.

Grissom, K. B., and L. A. Shepard. 1989. "Repeating and Dropping Out of School." In *Flunking Grades: Research and Policies on Retention*, ed. L. A. Shepard and M. L. Smith, 34–63. Philadelphia, Pa.: Falmer Press.

Hartocollis, A. 1999. "Miscalculation on Scores Shows a Weakness of Tests." *New York Times*, 17 September.

Hauser, R. M. 1999. *Should We End Social Promotion? Truth and Consequences*. Working Paper No. 99–06. Madison: Center for Demography and Ecology, University of Wisconsin.

Holmes, C. T. 1989. "Grade-Level Retention Effects: A Meta-Analysis of Research Studies." In *Flunking Grades: Research and Policies on Retention*, ed. L. A. Shepard and M. L. Smith, 34–63. Philadelphia, Pa.: Falmer Press.

Holmes, C. T., and K. M. Mathews. 1984. "The Effects of Nonpromotion on Elementary and Junior High School Pupils: A Meta-Analysis." *Review of Educational Research* 54, no. 2, 225–36.

House, E. 1989. "Policy Implications of Retention Research." In *Flunking Grades: Research and Policies on Retention*, ed. L. A. Shepard and M. L. Smith, 202–13. Philadelphia, Pa.: Falmer Press.

Kelly, K. 1999. "Retention vs. Social Promotion: Schools Search for Alternatives." *Harvard Education Letter, Research Online.* www.edletter.org/past/issues/1999-jf/retention.shtml (accessed 12 August 2002).

McCollum, P., A. Cortez, O. H. Maroney, and F. Montes. 1999. "Failing Our Children: Finding Alternatives to In-Grade Retention." Policy Brief. San Antonio, Tex.: Intercultural Development Research Association.

Meisels, S. J., and F. Liaw. 1993. "Failure in Grade: Do Students Catch Up?" *Journal of Educational Research* 50, no. 2, 69–77.

National Research Council. 1998. *High Stakes: Testing for Tracking, Promotion, and Graduation*. Washington, D.C.: National Academy Press.

Roderick, M. 1995. "Grade Retention and School Dropout: Policy Debate and Research Questions." *Phi Delta Research Bulletin*, no. 15, 1–6.

Romey, W. 2000. "A Note on Social Promotion." *Phi Delta Kappan* 81, no. 8, 632.

Shepard, L. A., and M. L. Smith, eds. 1989. *Flunking Grades: Research and Policies on Retention*. Philadelphia, Pa.: Falmer Press.

Shepard, L. A., and M. L. Smith. 1990. "Repeating Grades in School: Current Practice and Research Evidence." Policy Brief. New Brunswick, N.J.: Center for Policy Research in Education.

"State Officials Say Math Tests Too Easy." 2001. *Wilmington Star News*, 24 May.

Texas Education Agency. 2001. "Grade Level Retention." www.tea.state.tx.us/reports/1996cmprpt/04retain.html (accessed 15 July 2002).

Walters, D. M., and S. B. Borgers. 1995. "Student Retention: Is It Effective?" *School Counselor* 42, no. 4, 300–310.

Westchester Institute for Human Services Research. 2001. "The Balanced View: Social Promotion and Retention." www.sharingsuccess.org/code/socprom.html (accessed 15 July 2002).

Yamamoto, K. 1980. "Children under Stress: The Causes and Cures." Family Weekly, *Ogden Standard Examiner*, 6–8 September.

Chapter Eight

Who Will Teach? Testing and the Teaching Profession

I have seen some of the most bubbly teachers in this school . . . in this system and probably in the state, lose that enthusiasm, that zest they had for teaching [as a result of the testing]. [I have] seen a lot of good teachers leave already, and I'm afraid the numbers are going to become more massive. I think that's when they are going to open their eyes when they see teachers walking out by the droves. (Yarbrough, 1999, p. 86)

The existing teacher shortage in many areas of the country is expected to become even more critical over the next several years. With the increase in the number of school-age children and the high number of baby-boomer teachers retiring, it will become important not only to attract new teachers into the profession, but also to retain the existing teachers. There is a concern among some educators that high-stakes testing will drive many capable teachers out of teaching (e.g., Kohn, 2000). In this chapter, we discuss why some educators have made this claim and examine whether the claim has merit.

TEACHERS' CAREER DECISIONS

Teachers leave the teaching profession for a variety of reasons, including (in no particular order): high stress (i.e., tension, frustration, anxiety, anger, depression); low salary; lack of influence over school policy; a sense of collegial isolation; student-related factors (e.g., diversity in needs, too many students, disruptive students); poor working conditions (e.g., inadequate materials); inadequate administrative support (from central office and principals); personal circumstances (e.g., pregnancy/

137

childrearing, family relocation, marriage); lack of career advancement opportunities; and lack of respect and recognition. Billingsley (1993) developed a conceptual model of the factors that influence teachers' career decisions. This model identifies and organizes many of the major factors affecting a teacher's decision to stay or leave the teaching profession. Among the factors that influence career decisions are the "work conditions," including district policies, school environments, and the nature of teachers' individual work assignments. As Billingsley explains:

> It is hypothesized that qualified teachers working in desirable environments will have greater opportunities to experience work rewards (e.g., professional fulfillment, recognition, salary). These rewards should lead to increased levels of commitment (e.g., to school, district, teaching field, and profession) and lead to decisions to stay in teaching. However, when professional qualifications and work conditions are not as favorable, teachers are likely to experience fewer rewards and, thus, reduced commitment. Whether teachers actually leave depends on a host of personal, social, and economic factors. (Billingsley, 1993, pp. 146–147)

To apply Billingsley's model, it is necessary to assess the effects of high-stakes tests on a teacher's work environment. If high-stakes tests create undesirable working conditions, then the model predicts that teachers will experience reduced commitment and possibly leave the teaching profession, depending upon the complex interaction of the other factors in the model.

There is evidence that high-stakes testing has negatively affected some teachers' work environments. As a study of principals found:

> The increased emphasis on testing and the stakes associated with student and teacher performance on tests have caused some teachers to reconsider how long they want to remain teachers. Some of the principals believed they would be losing some of their best teachers, and as a result were concerned about the future strength of the educational programs in their schools. (Danielson, 1999, p. 171)

To understand how testing can negatively affect a teacher's work environment, we will discuss three major categories of negative effects on teachers' work environments that are described in research. First, teachers have more job stress because of the pressure they feel for their students to perform well on the tests. Second, teachers have less autonomy in making decisions about issues that affect their work conditions. Finally, teachers feel less respected as professionals. Each of these categories is discussed in the ensuing sections; finally, we present a section on the effects of testing on teacher recruitment at lower-performing schools.

More Job Stress

In a survey, 88 percent of teachers agreed that they were under "undue pressure" to improve students' test scores (Koretz et al., 1996). Similarly, 76 percent of teachers surveyed in one study (Jones et al., 1999) and more than two-thirds of educators in another (Elliott, 2000) reported that their jobs were more stressful since the implementation of high-stakes testing. (We use the term "stress" in this chapter in the same manner that Kyriacou [1989] described it: as the experience of tension, frustration, anxiety, anger, and depression resulting from work.) One teacher explained, "A few years ago, I really loved teaching, but this pressure is just so intense . . . I'm not sure how long I can take it" (Barksdale-Ladd and Thomas, 2000, p. 390). Clearly, this teacher is weighing stress as an important factor in her decision to stay in teaching.

In New York City the pressure is even more intense at the fourth grade level, because that is the grade in which the high-stakes tests are given in elementary school. One fourth grade teacher in the Bronx reported, "I need to not feel that intense pressure that if the kids don't improve, our school will be closed down. . . . I need a break so I can recover my strength" (Goodnough, 2001, p. A29).

Principals have also noted the increased levels of stress felt by teachers at their schools. In one study, a principal "believed her teachers were working hard and shouldering greater amounts of stress in order to meet the expectations of the state" (Danielson, 1999, p. 64). However, the stress might be too great for some teachers, and this principal "was concerned that teachers may leave the teaching field altogether due to the 'stress of the [high-stakes tests]'" (p. 64). A principal in Brooklyn said that the fourth grade teachers in his school have told him that high-stakes testing is "giving them health problems and high blood pressure" (Goodnough, 2001, p. A29).

On the other hand, most jobs do have a healthy amount (or more) of stress. Shouldn't teachers be expected to feel some pressure to do a competent job? In fact, it is likely that some teachers didn't feel enough pressure to improve teaching prior to the testing movement. For these teachers, the added stress might have been the positive pressure that they needed to reassess their practices. A principal in Danielson's (1999) study found that the testing "provided the 'leverage' needed to move some teachers who were not 'risk takers' into seeing the necessity for change. Not only can the [testing] become the 'catalyst for change,' [the principal] believed it could also 'support the change process'" (p. 75). In this case, the testing pressures resulted in what the principal saw as a positive change.

These findings are consistent with motivation theories that suggest that when individuals are underchallenged, higher performance standards can provide a "positive, productive, challenge-based stress" that will increase the individual's performance (Reeve, 1996, p. 192). If, however, the standards are overly challenging and unreasonably difficult, then the individual experiences an "anxious, unproductive, threat-based stress" (Reeve, 1996, p. 192). Because teachers across the nation experience different levels of stress from their states, school districts, principals, fellow teachers, and students' parents, and because teachers vary in their quality of teaching, there are undoubtedly some teachers that will fall into each of these conditions. That is, the added pressure likely has positive effects on some teachers and negative effects on others. Understanding this phenomenon helps one to understand that this is not a black and white issue and that the stress must be interpreted within the context of the situation. Unfortunately, there appear to be at least some teachers in school districts with high-stakes tests who feel an anxious, unproductive, and threat-based stress that leads to an undesirable working condition. According to Billingsley's (1993) model, this condition can set the stage for teachers to leave the profession.

Less Autonomy

In the same way that autonomy is important for a student's level of motivation and enjoyment (as described in chapter 5), autonomy is also important for a teacher's level of enjoyment and satisfaction in his or her job. That is, teachers have the need to be self-determining and autonomous within their job environment, and thus, they need to have a measure of control over their actions and have input into decisions that affect their jobs.

Several studies have provided evidence to back this claim. For instance, four hundred past national and state Teachers of the Year were surveyed and asked, "What do experienced teachers need to encourage them to remain in the classroom?" (Council of Chief State School Officers, 2000, p. 8). Seventy-three percent of the teachers reported that there was a "great need" for these teachers to have an active role in school decision making. As one teacher explained, "Teachers who do not believe they are active participants in the decision-making process become frustrated, disillusioned, and . . . tend to leave the profession" (Council of Chief State School Officers, 2000, p. 8).

These teachers' sentiments were echoed in a study that used data from two National Center for Education Statistics national surveys designed to investigate teacher attrition in public schools (Shen, 1997). One of the four policy implications that were developed based on the results of the study was to empower teachers. More specifically, the study reported:

> Teachers are traditionally not given much decision power. However, the data of this study clearly indicate that teachers who feel having more influence over school and teaching policies are more likely to stay. To empower teachers is one of the ways to improve teacher retention. (Shen, 1997, p. 38)

Has high-stakes testing given teachers this autonomy and empowerment that enhances their retention? Unfortunately, the answer appears to be no. In contrast, some teachers believe that high-stakes testing has curtailed their autonomy (e.g., Berger and Elson, 1996). For instance, teachers in Texas were asked: "It has also been suggested that the emphasis on TAAS [Texas Assessment of Academic Skills] is forcing some of the best teachers to leave teaching because of the restraints the tests place on decision making and the pressures placed on them and their students. Do you agree or disagree?" (Hoffman, Assaf, and Paris, 2001). In response, 85 percent of the teachers agreed with this statement, while only 15 percent disagreed. Clearly, teachers in Texas believe that less autonomy and more stress is leading to an increase in teacher attrition.

In a study designed to assess the impacts of the re-institution of twelfth grade final exams in British Columbia, Canada, Wideen et al. (1997) interviewed and observed teachers in grades eight, ten, and twelve in addition to principals, students, and district personnel. They reported, "On the basis of this analysis, we concluded that the policy of re-introducing school-leaving examinations has undermined the notion of teacher as autonomous professional" (p. 440).

Some teachers reported that they were less creative in their teaching (as we discussed in chapter 3). The result was that some teachers claimed that instruction had been reduced to "a cookbook kind of approach" in order to get high scores on the tests (Perreault, 2000, p. 708) and that they felt like robots who simply followed prescribed procedures (Barksdale-Ladd and Thomas, 2000, p. 392). Clearly, these teachers feel less autonomous than they did prior to the introduction of high-stakes testing. As one teacher explained:

> I didn't need a college degree and a master's degree to do what I do now. They don't need real teachers to prepare children for tests and, in fact, I think they

could just develop computer programs to do this. (Barksdale-Ladd and Thomas, 2000, p. 392)

A teacher in another study was frustrated with her lack of autonomy and commented:

> Before [the state testing program], you know, I could just go with the kids if something came up which hooked them. But now if we just start off in a different direction, I get worried we won't get back to what's required, and I have to kind of rein them in. I know they get frustrated, and I sure do. I think, well, is this what I got into teaching for? (Perreault, 2000, p. 707)

As a whole, these studies suggest that teachers need to be empowered and have autonomy over their actions and over the decisions that affect them in order to be satisfied with their jobs, and that a high-stakes testing environment can take that empowerment and autonomy away. As a result, teachers have yet another reason to be dissatisfied with their work environment.

Less Respect as Professionals

After surveying four hundred national and state Teachers of the Year from across the country, the Council of Chief State School Officers (2000) concluded, "Perhaps what our preeminent educators most clearly expressed in the survey is that *respect* is a precondition for addressing the challenges of recruitment and retention" (emphasis added, p. 9). Unfortunately, many teachers are insulted by the lack of respect they are receiving and the manner in which their profession is being affected by the high-stakes testing:

> These tests, and all of this pressure to make kids do well on the tests . . . it's an insult. It's saying that we aren't a profession and we can't be trusted to do our jobs, so high-pressure tactics are necessary to make us behave. They're treating us like stupid children, they're turning us into bad teachers, taking away every bit of pride. (Barksdale-Ladd and Thomas, 2000, p. 392)

We asked a former teacher whether the high-stakes testing made her feel like less of a professional and contributed to her leaving the profession after only teaching for two years. She responded, "Feeling like less of a professional is an understatement" and added, "I don't want to be appreciated, I want to be valued for my skill."

To add insult to injury, some states have mandated or threatened that teachers at lower-performing schools would be required to take a teacher competency exam to remain certified. This threat has struck a chord with many teachers, who resent the lack of respect that this exam suggests. A principal in Danielson's (1999) study noted: "We've had a lot of teachers upset at the prospect of them having to take a test which [will occur] later on in the year. Many of them have been teaching a long time . . . and they said they would take the test and then they would quit teaching . . . and I think they mean it. . . . I have a lot of people [who] are really good teachers" (p. 170). In short, testing has made some teachers feel less respected as professional educators.

EFFECTS ON
LOWER-PERFORMING SCHOOLS

Lower-performing schools can have an especially difficult time in recruiting and retaining quality teachers. Lower-performing schools are often composed of higher percentages of poor students who generally need more help to succeed in school. Although some teachers enjoy working with the lower-performing poor students, many prefer not to. As a result, several principals have reported concern about their ability to recruit teachers in lower-performing schools (Danielson, 1999). As one superintendent noted, "Teachers don't want to work in those schools" (Hui, 2002, p. 8A). (This superintendent also noted, though, that there are exceptions.) The consequence is that the neediest students are often taught by the least qualified, experienced, and academically-skilled teachers (Wayne, 2002). In the medical field, this would be analogous to wanting everyone to be healthy and then sending the people with the most serious and complex illnesses to the worst-trained and least experienced physicians. This type of strategy makes little sense in the field of medicine or education. Schools need well-trained and experienced teachers for all students.

This condition is made more critical in states that offer incentives to teachers at the highest-rated schools. A principal in North Carolina commented:

> How are you going to get somebody to go to a *Low Performing* school . . . when they could get offered a job at an [*Exemplary* school]. . . . At [the *Exemplary* school] they have a decent chance at getting a $1500 bonus each year, and at that other school not very much of a chance at getting a $1500 bonus. And teachers that are . . . at a high performing school for three or four years [are] going to make $6,000 more dollars [*sic*]! (Danielson, 1999, p. 52)

(Note: In North Carolina, teachers are given a $1,500 bonus if their school is ranked highly.)

Incentives can also affect the *retention* of teachers at a lower-performing school. Slightly more than half of the teachers surveyed in one study reported that they would consider changing schools if their school was designated in the lowest category (Jones et al., 1999). Morse (2000) reported, "Colorado has already seen a flurry of resignations and transfer requests [due to the tests] by teachers in its poorer pockets" (p. 36). Mandated teacher exams for teachers at lower-performing schools will likely only exacerbate this problem, because teachers will seek jobs at higher-performing schools where they can avoid taking the test. Thus, even when these teachers stay in the teaching profession, there will be a disproportionately negative effect on lower-performing schools.

CONCLUSION

There is merit to the claim that the implementation of high-stakes testing programs may be associated with increased rates of teacher attrition. The reasons for this include more job stress, less autonomy, and less professional respect. However, we want to be clear that we do not see high-stakes testing as the sole reason for teachers leaving the profession. Instead, the tests add to an already lengthy list of reasons that cause teachers to decide to leave the profession. As one teacher who recently left the profession explained, "To say we leave just because of the tests wouldn't be the whole picture, but it adds to the stress and low salary. It's the cherry on the sundae."

REFERENCES

Barksdale-Ladd, M. A., and K. F. Thomas. 2000. "What's at Stake in High-Stakes Testing: Teachers and Parents Speak Out." *Journal of Teacher Education* 51, 384–87.

Berger, N., and H. H. Elson. 1996. "What Happens When MCTs Are Used As an Accountability Device: Effects on Teacher Autonomy, Cooperation, and School Mission." Paper presented at the annual meeting of the American Educational Research Association, New York, April.

Billingsley, B. S. 1993. "Teacher Retention and Attrition in Special and General Education: A Critical Review of the Literature." *Journal of Special Education* 27, 137–74.

Council of Chief State School Officers. 2000. *Teacher Voices 2000: A Survey on Teacher Recruitment and Retention.* Washington, D.C.: Scholastic, Inc.

Danielson, M. L. 1999. "How Principals Perceive and Respond to a High-Stakes Accountability Measure." Abstract in *Dissertation Abstracts International* 61, 03A (UMI No. 9967692).

Elliott, J. 2000. *NCAE Issues Recommendations to Improve ABCs Accountability Plan.* www.ncae.org/news/000717pr.shtml (accessed 18 April 2002).

Goodnough, A. 2001. "High Stakes of Fourth-Grade Tests Are Driving Off Veteran Teachers." *New York Times*, 14 June, A1, A29.

Hoffman, J. V., L. Assaf, and S. G. Paris. 2001. "High Stakes Testing in Reading: Today in Texas, Tomorrow?" *Reading Teacher* 54, no. 5, 482–92.

Hui, T. K. 2002. "Teacher Picture is Grim." *The News and Observer*, 2 July, 1A, 8A.

Jones, G. M., B. D. Jones, B. H. Hardin, L. Chapman, T. Yarbrough, and M. Davis. 1999. "The Impact of High-Stakes Testing on Teachers and Students in North Carolina." *Phi Delta Kappan* 81, 199–203.

Kohn, A. 2000. "Standardized Testing and Its Victims." *Education Week* 20 (27 September): 46–47.

Koretz, D., K. Mitchell, S. Barron, and S. Keith. 1996. *Final Report: Perceived Effects of the Maryland School Performance Assessment Program* (CSE Tech. Rep. No. 409). Los Angeles: University of California, National Center for Research on Evaluation, Standards, and Student Testing (CRESST).

Kyriacou, C. 1989. "Teacher Stress and Burnout: An International Review." In *Human Resource Management in Education*, ed. C. Riches and C. Morgan, 60–68. Milton Keynes, U.K.: Open University Press.

Morse, J. 2000. "Is That Your Final Answer?" *Time* 155, no. 25 (19 June): 34–38.

Perreault, G. 2000. "The Classroom Impact of High-Stakes Testing." *Education* 120, 705–10.

Reeve, J. 1996. *Motivating Others: Nurturing Inner Motivational Resources.* Boston: Allyn and Bacon.

Shen, J. 1997. "How to Reduce Teacher Attrition in Public Schools: Policy Implications from a National Study." *Educational Horizons* 76, 33–39.

Wayne, A. 2002. "Teacher Inequality: New Evidence on Disparities in Teachers' Academic Skills." *Education Policy Analysis Archives* 10, no. 30 (13 June). epaa.asu.edu/epaa/v10n30/ (accessed 2 August 2002).

Wideen, M. F., T. O'Shea, I. Pye, and G. Ivany. 1997. "High-Stakes Testing and the Teaching of Science." *Canadian Journal of Education* 22, 428–44.

Yarbrough, T. L. 1999. "Teacher Perceptions of the North Carolina ABC Program and the Relationship to Classroom Practice." Ph.D. dissertation, University of North Carolina at Chapel Hill.

Chapter Nine

Stepping up to the Plate: Symbols of Testing

The language associated with high-stakes testing is packed with analogies that instantly bring forth images that are common across our culture. Americans talk about "high stakes," "rewards," "standards," and "performance" in relation to testing, and without further explanation or elaboration these symbols cross our common understandings and shape our interpretations. The power of these images emerges as they elicit conscious and unconscious reactions without the benefit of two-way communication (Trifonas, 2001).

As Americans, our lives are so filled with the signs and symbols of our culture that we scarcely notice the baggage that these symbols carry. We move through a world of McDonald's arches, Nike swooshes, and Disney mouse ears. The media and advertising industries count on this power of analogy to alter our motivations and actions. Not surprisingly, testing reform is intentionally embedded in carefully selected symbolism that is intended to arouse public opinion and influence the direction of the testing movement.

What are our nation's images of testing, and how do these images shape our interpretations of testing policy? More importantly, beyond the surface of the symbols, what are the underlying messages and the hidden assumptions that are embedded in the language of testing? Airasian (1988) argues: "symbols tend to be evocative rather than analytical, emotional rather than intellectual . . . evoke not only concrete images, but also feelings, values, emotions, and sentiments" (p. 302). Before a movement like high-stakes testing gains acceptance, Airasian suggests that the educational innovation is first filtered through the symbols of broader social values. A close look at the rhetoric of testing (table 9.1) shows the power of the imagery and language used to associate testing with sets of values and beliefs that people want from public education.

THE ONE-ROOM SCHOOLHOUSE

One of the most persistent images in American education is the one-room schoolhouse. In fact, Texas uses this image in its testing logo.

The one-room schoolhouse brings to mind a nostalgic view of education in pioneer days when schools were small and safe and a homogenous set of students all knew each other and the teacher. This image also suggests students working to learn the essentials of reading, writing, and arithmetic. When politicians refer to "the basics," "rewards," "ABCs," and students working with their "noses to the grindstone," the language suggests another time when life was perceived as simpler, when there was a single devoted teacher who taught the essential subjects along with the values of hard work. The symbolic values associated with the image include a focus on families, community, simplicity, order, safety, small

Table 9.1   Metaphors of Testing

Metaphor	Elicited Images	Language of Testing
One-Room Schoolhouse	safety, discipline, order, familiarity, simplicity, basics, family, reading, writing, and arithmetic	Back to the basics Rewards Punishment
Ball Game	competition, win/lose, some play/others can't, public event, pleasure, all-stars, champion	Measure up Step up to the plate Coming up to bat Winners and losers Prizes Performance Number one Raise the bar
Factory	manufacturing, quality control, production line, raw materials, rejects, deadlines, products, recycling	Making the grade Ratchet up the pressure Low-performing Retention Gateway Nose to the grindstone
Disneyland/Pleasantville	uniformity, cleanliness, families, standardization, familiarity	Standards All children at grade level

classes, and a teacher who was responsive to parents. Although these are desirable traits of schools, the analogy is problematic because it fails to recognize the complexity of our nation's society and our educational systems. Schools are no longer small; many elementary school populations exceed 1,000 students, and it isn't unusual for middle and high schools to serve thousands of students each day. Most modern schools serve diverse multicultural communities in which several languages are spoken and that bear little resemblance to the uniform cultures of the one-room schoolhouses in the prairie towns of bygone days. Within a single family, children may ride buses across town to different schools separated by many miles. Parents' desires to have small, responsive schools where their children are well known and where parents' interests are respected is an important goal, but high-stakes testing does nothing to address the complex issues of school size, a transient and mobile population, and school culture.

THE BALL GAME

Some of the most pervasive symbols of our culture emerge from sports. What is more American than baseball, mom, and apple pie? Sports metaphors abound in testing. Politicians, parents, and educators often talk about testing using expressions such as "stepping up to the plate," "coming up to bat," "winning or losing," "measuring up," or being "number one." Associated with these images are notions of schooling as a competitive endeavor, testing as a public event with winners and losers, and the presence of teams on which only those who pass the "tryout" get to "play." For many people, the sports metaphor suggests hard work, dedication, and perseverance to stay in the game. These are all desirable values from a public perspective. But the analogy of education as a ball game falls short in a variety of places. Perhaps most importantly, the sports metaphor fails because education is not a game with winners and losers. Unlike sports, schools can't pick who is on the team and who sits out, nor can schools exclude the less "fit" or the unmotivated.

Educators strive for all students to be winners, but the testing-by-reform movement has created new categories of students and large numbers of people who will be labeled winners and losers. Each year this labeling process begins anew, and as the losers improve their "performance," the "bar" is raised so that new categories of winners and losers can be created. (See chapter 5 for a discussion of the impact of labeling students' competence motivation). The labels of winners and losers now apply to school systems, schools, principals, teachers, and students at every level of the educational hierarchy. Tied to the titles of winners and losers are the symbols of rewards, sanctions, and penalties. These take the form of financial inducements dangled in front of underpaid educators, or negative actions such as public embarrassment (which brings to mind the Pilgrims' practice of locking people into stocks in the public square), mandatory assistance teams, or the threat of takeover by the state. This tendency to compare and rank ourselves is a strong American practice that is embedded in our daily culture (Kohn, 1992). We take pride at "beating out the other guy" and being "better" than others. But within schools, we cannot afford to have losers.

Educators, recognizing the gaming aspects of testing, often learn how to play to win. Across the United States, educators have scheduled pep rallies before testing events, have fed the "players" extra nutritious breakfasts before the tests, and have held repeated warm-ups, practice sessions, and strategy sessions to figure out how to "win." We can't pick and choose who comes to school and who does not (although there are those who would like to exclude the slow "runners"). Schools must serve all children, not just those who are particularly healthy, talented, or highly motivated.

The language that designates winners and losers falls short of usefulness when children are our focus. These children are winners and losers at what? As complex human beings, we each hold a range of talents and skills. One person may excel in reading, while another is talented in mathematics or painting. The range of these skills within a single grade level is vast, and although one student might be able to write a novel, another might struggle to write a single paragraph. Looking a little closer, we recognize that the struggling writer may be an accomplished musician. So what defines winning? To sum up the diversity of human talents into a single test score (which most likely measures a narrow range of skills) is to fail to recognize the wonderful complexity that constitutes humanity.

Education is not a ball game where children can choose to play or not. We can't select our teams, or decide in which innings we will put our best players. We can't allow any student to "strike out" or "sit on the bench." This is also not a betting sport in which wealthy spectators sit on the sideline and watch to see which teams will get to the playoffs and which teams will go down in the first round. The stakes are too high for this metaphor, and Americans must strip away the rhetoric of the language of sports to put human lives at the center of our focus.

THE FACTORY

"School cannot be a place of pleasure, with all the freedom that would imply. School is a factory, and we need to know which workers are up to snuff . . . everything, absolutely everything in the school setting—enforces the competitive nature of the institution, itself a model of the workaday world" (Pennac, 1994, p. 92).

The manufacturing analogy of education emerges consistently whenever leaders from business and industry lead educational reform. Terms like "ratchet up the pressure," "production of literate citizens," "productivity," "beating last year's goals," and changing the "standard" suggest that schools are a factory with the task of producing a product that will serve business and industry (Serafini, 2002). The imagery suggests visions of neat, orderly assembly lines where students are the raw materials and quality control is conducted periodically. If one of the "products" fails to meet standards, then the product (the student) is recycled through the production line until it meets standards. The goal is for the production process to efficiently meet deadlines and produce a uniform product that meets all measures of quality.

It is easy to see how schools, particularly the very large schools that have evolved in recent years, are viewed as factories. School systems have "warehoused" and "moved students along" as if they were anonymous products. Even graduation ceremonies suggest that each of the uniformly wrapped individuals comes with a guarantee of standard quality. Standardization, of course, is exactly what some employers want. Since a good economy is dependent on having trained workers who can fill assembly lines, human resources that can be counted on to improve the efficiency and productivity of business are most valued.

This view of children as raw materials is where educators diverge dramatically from leaders in business and industry. Educators do not typically view themselves as producing workers for industry, but that is exactly what some business leaders want from our educational system. The tension around this point of view threatens to break any effort to significantly reform education. Teachers look at the students in their classes as diverse and rich human beings whose lives are likely to go in a myriad of directions. They seek to develop the wide range of talents and skills that each child possesses. It is morally incomprehensible to most educators to repeatedly label a child as below standard and to send him or her back time and time again, because it is ineffective to do so (as we discussed in chapter 7). Teachers know that children arrive at school with huge disparities in abilities, home resources, and past experiences and that these elements will define how a child progresses at school. Reform by testing is typically blind to the differences children have as they enter schooling. These differences, however, are not trivial. They must be considered in providing each child with a quality education. High-stakes testing is designed to get short-term gains without addressing the fundamental inequities that exist among children, families, and schools. The factory model of schooling drags along assumptions that get in the way of meaningful reform of education.

DISNEYLAND/PLEASANTVILLE

Disney is a powerful American icon that we in this country are increasingly adopting as our community goal (Giroux, 1999). Housing developments are sprouting up across the nation that mimic the Disney town of Celebration, Florida or the town in the movie *Pleasantville*. In these planned communities, homes are built with similar layouts, are painted with a narrow range of colors, have yards of a designated size, and are devoid of the products of human activities such as clotheslines, unused bicycles, yard art, and children's playground equipment. Trash cans, lawn mowers, and items such as paint cans are required by the homeowner covenants to be hidden out of sight.

The Disney image brings to mind the small town of yesteryear, a place of fun and innocence, where there is no garbage, crime, or illness. Instead, the town is filled with efficient technology and maintained by an army of attractive, smiling young people.

On the surface, schools that resembled Disneyland would appear to be wonderful places to educate children. The attractiveness of the Disney symbolism is fueled by parents' concerns about school safety, struggles with underfunded and poorly maintained buildings, and fear of the rapidly changing demographics of school populations. According to Trifonas (2001), the Disney ideology "depends on a conception of an interpretive community as the abode of subjects who are the same, and without difference, think the same, hold the same desires, values, and ideals" (p. 24). It is an ideal place of innocence and uniformity.

Unlike many of our parents' and grandparents' schools, schools today are often filled with children who speak limited or no English, don't celebrate familiar holidays, and do not attend the neighborhood churches or synagogues. "No nation on earth has ever tried to educate the diverse student population that attends America's schools today. No educational system has ever tried to provide *academic* instruction to the range of students enrolled in schools today. Add to this complexity all the ills—dysfunctional families, high rates of student turnover and absenteeism, community violence, substance abuse, teen pregnancy—that have a powerful effect on academic motivation and involvement" (McLaughlin, 1991, p. 250). It is no wonder we long for the Disney image of clean, efficient, innocent, and safe schools. But looking a little deeper, do we really want our schools to resemble the Disney town of Celebration, "a predominately White middle-class community where public behavior is heavily regulated in order to inculcate the appearance of similitude and homogeneity, a non-offending environment of good sense and sensibility" (Trifonas, 2001, p. 27)?

Do we really want to wipe away color, remove variation, and make our schools uniform places where students are all expected to meet the same standard at the same point in time? Could we do so even if we wanted to? Or is it our color and the myriad of shades of people, ideas, and perspectives that makes the United States great?

WHERE METAPHORS FAIL

While each of these metaphors for education falls short of representing the reality of our schools, the underlying values and beliefs provide insight into the goals of those who seek to reform education through testing. The visions of the one-room schoolhouse, the ball game, the factory, and Disney portray a time when life was less complex, when children were safe, and when families were valued. The pace of American lives and the complexity of our nation's rapidly changing demographics have left many afraid of change and leery of the unfamiliar. Some of these images, such as the one-room schoolhouse, suggest that the public wants schools that are familiar and secure. If schools can seriously look at the underlying issues that frame reform-by-testing efforts and can consider alternative ways to address the issues of complexity and uncertainty in schools, then perhaps educators can regain some of the trust needed to reform education in ways that will ensure quality education for all students.

REFERENCES

Airasian, P. 1988. "Symbolic Validation: The Case of State-Mandated, High-Stakes Testing." *Educational Evaluation and Policy Analysis* 10, no. 4, 302.

Giroux, H. 1999. *The Mouse that Roared: Disney and the End of Innocence.* Lanham, Md.: Rowman & Littlefield.

Kohn, A. 1992. *No Contest: The Case against Competition.* Boston: Houghton Mifflin.

McLaughlin, M. 1991. "Test-Based Accountability as a Reform Strategy." *Phi Delta Kappan* 73, no. 3, 248–51.

Pennac, D. 1994. *Better than Life.* Toronto: Coach House Press.

Serafini, F. 2002. "Dismantling the Factory Model of Assessment." *Reading and Writing Quarterly* 18, 67–85.

Trifonas, P. 2001. "Simulations of Culture: Disney and the Crafting of American Popular Culture." *Educational Researcher* 30, no. 1, 23–28.

Chapter Ten

Reforming the Reform

In its current form, high-stakes testing is not the panacea for all of the problems with public education. In fact, the unintended consequences that have arisen due to the tests' implementation have brought about their own unique problems and complications. However, due to the great political support for the testing, it is unlikely that that it will end anytime soon. In fact, the No Child Left Behind Act of 2001 signed into law by President Bush in January 2002 requires testing in reading and writing for all students in grades three through eight. For some states, this will require the development of new tests or the modification of existing tests. As Jones and Whitford (1997) explained, "While some educational leaders privately acknowledge that the high-stakes system has had unintended, dysfunctional consequences, they quickly add that the political environment will not permit them to back away from it" (pp. 280–81). Unfortunately, as we have described in this book, the unintended negative consequences of testing are too great to ignore. What then, can be done when designing testing programs to avoid many of the unintended consequences that we have discussed in this book?

In this chapter, we provide a summary of some of the most critical reform items that need immediate attention and possible approaches for change (American Educational Research Association [AERA], 2000; Commission on Instructionally Supportive Assessment, 2001). If accountability systems can incorporate more of these suggestions, then the unintended side effects can be reduced and meaningful change in education can move forward.

FOCUS ON LEARNING

One of the goals of testing should be to improve student learning. Many parents, politicians, and administrators fall into the trap of thinking that student achievement on tests reflects what students know. But tests only measure a sample of what students learn. Keeping *learning* as the focus reminds us that *achievement* is not the goal. Achievement in public education is traditionally defined as what can be measured through tests, whereas learning is a complex endeavor that rarely lends itself to simple measurements. It is a strange reality that in many of today's high-stakes testing programs instruction, learning, and testing are "often conceived as curiously separate in time and purpose" (Graue, 1993, p. 291). Reminding ourselves that learning is at the heart of education keeps the teaching and learning process balanced (Hurwitz, 2000). The focus on learning also helps us to avoid falling into the trap of thinking about test scores as the goal, resulting in a richer view of schooling.

When we put learning first in the line of educational priorities, attention shifts to looking at and assessing the *development* of knowledge, not simply selected endpoints. This perspective allows us to acknowledge that the process of learning is complex, dynamic, and multidimensional. Learning occurs along a continuum that isn't always linear, and assessments that acknowledge the nature of knowledge development build into the assessment model multiple ways of assessing learning in different contexts and over longer periods of time.

From the students' perspective, such formative assessments would allow students to view learning as progress over time as opposed to portraying knowledge as something that they either have or don't have when they pass or fail a test. This perspective would provide failing students with the understanding that they have some knowledge and would allow them to realize that they can build upon this knowledge. This view contrasts with the view that if they don't pass the test, they lack sufficient intelligence, knowledge, or skills necessary to pass the test. Furthermore, the tests should provide diagnostic information that students, teachers, and parents can use to better understand the student's academic strengths and weaknesses. Although there is value in having summative data that can be used to look at the health of educational programs across schools and school districts, a better balance between formative (diagnostic) assessments and the traditional summative assessments given in statewide testing programs is needed.

AVOID ASSESSMENTS
ONLY FOR COMPARISONS

Although American schools are ingrained with competition, when test scores are used to primarily compare one school to another, the relationship of the test scores to learning grows more remote. Yet most high-stakes accountability programs are designed to reform schools by offering them up for public comparison. This shift in assessment goals from supporting learning to serving for public comparison fails to help students in meaningful ways. Although there are legitimate needs for administrators to have comparative assessment data to look across grades and schools for changes in student learning across time, the political comparisons of schools suggest that it is worth asking, Who benefits from this type of assessment reporting and why? The winners in these types of comparisons may only be the realtors and any others who seek to profit by using the assessment information to sell homes. Comparisons among schools and school districts are often meaningless, and scores tend to reflect differences in socioeconomic levels of the families and communities. In North Carolina, for example, it can usually be predicted that the highest scores will go to the relatively affluent university communities and that the lowest scores are usually found in the poor urban and rural areas of the state.

MONITOR THE TIME AND MONEY
TESTING TAKES FROM TEACHING

Time is a precious asset, and within the busy school day, time for learning continues to decrease. Students are being asked to take more tests in a huge array of subjects and contexts, including tests for physical fitness; tests for eyesight; and tests for reading, writing, mathematics, second languages, character development, anger management; as well as international tests and benchmark tests to predict the results of the end-of-grade tests. In some school systems, students spend entire weeks of instructional time taking tests. And during high-stakes testing days, many schools ask teachers to limit instruction and not give homework assignments. In addition to the time it takes to give the tests, we must factor in the large amount of time schools spend preparing students to take the tests. This preparation time for testing is time that is removed from the available time students have to learn new things in the instructional day. There is also a significant loss of time for teachers, who must prepare tests, check answer sheets, locate test proctors, and develop presentations and materials to educate parents and the public about the tests. The time that teachers and administrators spend on the testing programs is time taken away from other forms of educational planning. The typical school day is already reduced for a huge array of things such as

fund-raising, pep rallies, speakers, character education, violence prevention, peer mediation, fluoride treatments for teeth, yearbook sales, and
many other school activities. When all of these demands on the educational day are added up, the time left for instruction is severely limited.
For those who care about education, the time that is spent preparing for
and giving tests must be carefully monitored. The bottom line for educators has to be: Is it better for students to take another test, or is it more
important to use the time for instruction?

In addition to taking away time from instruction, testing takes away
money that could be used for other instructional purposes. The costs
associated with creating, administering, and grading the tests is increasing, especially as students in more grade levels are tested and as more
subjects (such as science) are included in the testing process. When
authentic assessments (such as portfolios and other assessments that
assess students' performance on "real-life" tasks) are included, the costs
are even higher for test development, administration, and scoring.

NEVER USE ONE TEST FOR
HIGH-STAKES DECISIONS

A single test is a poor judge of what a student knows, and one test cannot be validly used to determine whether or not students graduate, are
promoted, or have access to higher levels of learning. A single test lacks
the type of reliability and validity needed to accurately measure a student's aptitude, ability, or achievement (Lewis, 2000; North Carolina
School Psychology Association, 2001). Students should be given multiple opportunities to demonstrate what they know and should be provided with ample support and additional help when they do not appear
to be making progress. Multiple measures of students' learning provide
parents, teachers, and administrators with a more complete and accurate
profile of students' capabilities.

VALIDATE TESTS FOR
EACH SEPARATE USE

Policy makers must ensure that tests are used only for the purposes for
which they were designed. A single test is not a measure of a student's
worth, nor is it an indication of school quality. When the public is

allowed to misuse or misinterpret the validity of tests, the harm out-weighs the benefits of using a test.

The responsibility for defining the limitations of tests rests first with the psychometricians and testing administrators who develop and select tests. But it is also the responsibility of anyone who uses test scores to be knowledgeable about the limitations and boundaries of score infer-ences. This means that counselors, principals, and teachers must be dili-gent in making sure proper interpretations of tests are used. It also means that the educational community must demand that the media and the larger public use scores only for their validated purposes.

Moreover, tests should be used for high-stakes decisions only after they have been deemed sufficiently reliable and valid. Unfortunately, many states are trying to validate tests while using them for high-stakes decisions. This is like trying to build an airplane and fly it at the same time.

DISCLOSE POTENTIAL NEGATIVE CONSEQUENCES

Evaluating the effectiveness and consequences of testing programs is essential. Potential impacts of testing should be disclosed to participants and the public. Honest assessments of the impacts of testing allow test results to be used appropriately and keep abuses of testing to a mini-mum. Testing program evaluations allow educators and policy makers to weigh the benefits against the harm that may result in implementing a particular test. It is unacceptable to institute testing programs without serious consideration of the consequences of the assessment. The Ameri-can Educational Research Association's *Standards for Educational and Psychological Testing* state: "When unintended consequences result from test use, an attempt should be made to investigate whether such consequences arise from the test's sensitivity to characteristics other than those it is intended to assess or to the test's failure to fully represent the intended consequences" (1999, p. 23).

CREATE BETTER TESTS

Designing better tests that measure higher-order thinking skills, problem solving, and complex learning is critical if assessments are going to match instructional goals (e.g., Yeh, 2001). Educators must be more proactive in holding test designers accountable for tests that measure the types of learning described in curriculum standards. Furthermore, tests need to provide teachers with useful feedback so they can better help students in the specific areas in which they have low scores.

PROVIDE APPROPRIATE
ACCOMMODATIONS FOR STUDENTS
WITH SPECIAL NEEDS

Testing administrators must find ways to accommodate students with special needs in ways that are respectful and that honor their abilities. It is unacceptable for educators to suggest that some students should stay home on the day of the test, or to allow the scores of special needs students to block them from access to regular education programs. When scores are tied to promotion, testing policies take on a whole new light for students with special needs. One teacher of special education said in horror, "What am I supposed to tell my fifth graders who will never leave fifth grade because they can't pass the test?"

To address the needs of students with disabilities, Michigan has developed an alternate assessment program called MI-Access (Michigan Department of Education, 2002). This performance assessment relies upon teacher observation to assess students with cognitive impairments. This type of test addresses the need to assess students with disabilities in qualitatively different ways than other students. Instead of completing a written exam, "teachers watch students carry out a standard set of activities during the normal course of a school day and score them on a 1–4 scale" (Michigan Department of Education, 2002). This assessment process could prove to be a promising alternative to more common standardized tests.

ENSURE THAT TEACHERS HOLD
SIGNIFICANT ROLES IN THE DESIGN
OF ASSESSMENTS

Teachers must have significant roles in the design and development of assessments if tests are going to have any meaningful impact on instruction. In many areas, tests are developed by professional test developers and implemented by administrators, and teachers are often left completely out of the test development process. In some cases teachers are prohibited from even seeing the test items as students are taking the tests. Although we recognize the need for test validity and reliability, this artificial barrier between assessment and instruction does little to improve the quality of education in American schools.

Nebraska is in the process of designing a unique assessment system called School-based Teacher-led Assessment and Reporting System (STARS), which appears to address this problem to some extent. In this new assessment system, the state established the expectations and provided the leadership but also provided the local districts with choices about how they wished to assess their students. Each school district designed its own "district assessment plan," which included a balance of formative (classroom, teacher-designed) and summative (standardized, large-scale) assessments to measure the state standards. School districts are to be rated "according to how well they meet several specified criteria: percentages of students who meet the standards, quality of the assessments, and a challenge index for specified populations" (Roschewski, Gallagher, and Isernhagen, 2001, p. 613). This unique assessment system might provide a better balance of assessment and accountability than current tests in other states, because it includes a formative assessment component that could be used to provide more feedback about students' abilities.

SCREEN TESTING PROGRAMS FOR DEVELOPMENTAL APPROPRIATENESS

Educational research has provided a wealth of data about how children learn and how instruction can be sequenced and designed to best meet the developmental needs of children. Unfortunately, testing programs sometimes fail to promote developmentally appropriate instruction. In some cases the tests themselves are not developmentally appropriate for children. But in addition to the test instrument, the test preparation practices can be equally inappropriate. As we saw in one school, all the first graders were asked to sit on the floor repeating alphabet sounds for an hour each day. This system-wide, mandated, and scripted program failed to utilize what is known about children's attention spans, motivation, and physical needs and about the range of development that exists in a single classroom. We in the education field also know how variable student achievement is for young children, yet we continue to ask five- to eight-year-old children to sit and take paper-and-pencil standardized tests and then assume that the interpretations of these test scores have genuine meaning in telling us what children know and are able to do. Assessing young children isn't wrong, but it needs to be done in multiple formats, with reasonable time limits, and scores need to be used cautiously to make decisions about the education of a young child.

USE ALTERNATIVES TO STUDENT RETENTION

The research consistently shows that retention has significant negative impacts on students that outweigh any positive benefits (Hurwitz, 2000). Repeated studies show that students who are retained are more likely to drop out of school. Each time a student is retained increases the likelihood that the label of failure will become a permanent reality. As discussed in chapter 7, there are a variety of alternative models that allow students to progress along a continuum and do not necessitate repeatedly labeling students as failures. Instead, these alternative models assess progress continually and build on students' growth across time. Some students will need extra time to learn; some benefit from extended school days and summer remediation. The simple notion of retaining a student until mastery of a subject is met ignores the serious consequences that accompany retention.

There are numerous ways to creatively and effectively group students for instruction wherever they are in the learning continuum (e.g., American Association of School Administrators, 1992; Goodlad and Anderson, 1987; McClellan, 1994; Miller, 1995). In a number of schools, students whose learning is delayed are placed with other students who are at the same level, even if these students are a bit younger. For example, an eighth grade student may be in a general mathematics class composed of primarily sixth graders, but the same student may go over to the high school for an advanced writing class. Age is not necessarily a reliable indicator of the level of ideal achievement for students. A better model is to consider the range of a student's knowledge and skills and then develop a plan to meet that student's needs. Well-developed formative assessments can be invaluable in helping educators and parents design the best educational programs for children. Multiage and multigrade classes have a strong record of being successful with a wide range of learners. The critical difference in retention and multiage grouping is the underlying belief that students' learning is developmental, not necessarily chronological.

DEVELOP A VARIETY OF ASSESSMENTS
ALIGNED WITH GOALS

The primary goal of many public high-stakes assessments is to measure and promote an improvement in school quality. If the goal is to measure school effectiveness, there are a number of factors that parents and the public consider as important. These include areas such as school safety, dropout rates, teacher absentee rates, number of advanced placement courses offered for students, and teacher quality. If a school is going to be publicly judged, these are quality indicators that should be reported and considered. Recent history has shown that a school may have high achievement but otherwise have high levels of dropouts, abnormal amounts of competition, or high rates of student suicide and violence. Report cards on schools should reflect a variety of measures of school quality—not simply high-stakes test scores.

One strategy that has been reexamined is the use of school inspectors (Olson, 2001). School inspectors, like those that have been used in England, are local professionals who visit a school and identify the strengths and weaknesses of the school program. This inspection could result in public accountability for school improvement while involving the local community in correcting any problems that exist.

For student assessment, there are a number of ways to measure what students know and are able to do that go beyond the standardized test. Student portfolios, performance assessments, narrative evaluations, open-ended assessments, and clinical interviews are all useful tools in evaluating student learning. These methods of assessment help teachers and parents judge growth in authentic contexts and provide the types of feedback that can be useful to the student in setting new goals. These assessments focus on learning and not on comparisons of students, teachers, and schools. Research has shown that parents find report cards, graded examples of student work, and feedback from the teachers to be more useful than standardized test results (Shepard and Bleim, 1995).

BEYOND THE TESTS

These recommendations suggest a significant shift in perspective away from viewing scores as a goal and toward viewing learning as continual, complex, and individual. If the assessment focus is shifted from political arenas to the practical world of teaching children, then Americans can find ways to give communities, parents, teachers, and administrators the types of information that they need to help educate all our children. Administrators need assessment data that they can use to look at broad trends in learning across classes and schools, teachers need data to help them design learning environments, and parents need information about their children's progress. Clearly, educators need to open the schoolhouse doors to those who make policy and those who fund education. Educators need to invite the wider audiences of the public to join teachers and administrators in conversations about the challenges, demands, and problems of educating diverse groups of students in a global world. One of the insights that we have had while researching the field of assessment for this book is that there are very different views of the purposes of education held by different stakeholders. Until educators open this dialogue about the goal of schooling, then people from within and outside of the school will find themselves working against each other in ways that only frustrate efforts to reform and improve education.

REFERENCES

AERA (American Educational Research Association). 1999. *Standards for Educational and Psychological Testing*. Washington, D.C.: Author.

AERA (American Educational Research Association). 2000. "AERA Position Statement Concerning High-Stakes Testing in PreK–12 Education." aera.net/about/policy/stakes.htm (accessed 11 April 2002).

American Association of School Administrators. 1992. *The Nongraded Primary: Making Schools Fit Children*. Arlington, Va.: Author.

Commission on Instructionally Supportive Assessment. 2001. "Building Tests to Support Instruction and Accountability." October. www.nea.org/issues/highstakes/buildingtests.html (accessed 15 February 2002).

Goodlad, J. I., and R. H. Anderson. 1987. *The Nongraded Elementary School* (rev. ed.). New York: Teachers College Press.

Graue, M. E. 1993. "Integrating Theory and Practice through Instructional Assessment." *Educational Assessment* 1, 293–309.

Hurwitz, N. 2000. "Do High-Stakes Assessments Really Improve Learning?" *American School Board Journal* 187, no. 1, 20–25.

Jones, K., and B. L. Whitford. 1997. "Kentucky's Conflicting Reform Principles: High-Stakes Accountability and Student Performance Assessment." *Phi Delta Kappan* 78, 276–81.

Lewis, A. 2000. "Standing Firm on Standards." *Phi Delta Kappan* 82, no. 4, 263–64.

McClellan, D. E. 1994. "Multiage Grouping: Implications for Education." In *Full Circle: A New Look at Multiage Education*, ed. P. Chase and J. Doan, 147–66. Portsmouth, N.H.: Heinemann.

Michigan Department of Education. 2002. *MI-Access: Michigan's Alternative Assessment Program.* www.state.mi.us/mde/off/board/news/news022202.pdf (accessed 11 April 2002).

Miller, W. 1995. "Are Multiage Grouping Practices a Missing Link in the Educational Reform Debate?" *National Association of Secondary School Principals (NASSP) Bulletin,* February, 27–32.

North Carolina School Psychology Association. 2001. "Student Accountability Standards and High-Stakes Testing." Position Statement. www.ncpsy.org/SASPositionPaper.htm (accessed 21 January 2002).

Olson, L. 2001. "Moving beyond Test Scores." *Education Week on the Web.* www.edweek.org/sreports/qc99/ac/mc/mc9.htm (accessed 11 April 2002).

Roschewski, P., C. Gallagher, and J. Isernhagen. 2001. "Nebraskans Reach for the STARS." *Phi Delta Kappan* 82, 611–15.

Shepard, L., and C. Bleim. 1995. *Opinions Regarding Standardized Tests, Teacher's Information, and Performance Assessments.* Report No. CSE-TR-397. Los Angeles: National Center for Research on Evaluation, Standards, and Student Testing.

Yeh, S. S. 2001. "Tests Worth Teaching To: Constructing State-Mandated Tests that Emphasize Critical Thinking." *Educational Researcher* 30, no. 9, 12–17.

Chapter Eleven

Putting the Pieces Together

As someone who has spent his entire career doing research, writing, and thinking about educational testing and assessment issues, I would like to conclude by summarizing a compelling case showing that the major uses of tests for student and school accountability during the past 50 years have improved education and student learning in dramatic ways. Unfortunately, that is not my conclusion. Instead, I am led to conclude that in most cases the instruments and technology have not been up to the demands that have been placed on them by high-stakes accountability. Assessment systems that are useful monitors lose much of their dependability and credibility for that purpose when high stakes are attached to them. The unintended negative effects of the high-stakes accountability uses often outweigh the intended positive effects.

(Linn, 2000, p. 14)

The logic of high-stakes testing programs seems clear: they provide a mechanism to inform the public about school quality and to hold students and educators accountable. However, many of the intended consequences are not realized through current state accountability programs, and many of the unintended consequences are negative. As a result, it is imperative to weigh the pros and cons of testing to assess whether testing programs should be continued in their current form. The purpose of this book has been to provide evidence that can be used in making these decisions.

In this chapter, we present a summary of the intended and unintended consequences that were described throughout the book (see table 11.1). The consequences listed are derived from empirical research; case studies; surveys of teachers, principals, and the public; newspaper accounts; anecdotal accounts from parents, teachers, and administrators; and our own observations of testing programs in schools. This list should be interpreted with care, since it is not possible to determine the extent to which these consequences are found across schools, school systems, states, and, most importantly, testing programs. For instance, while one state has a testing program that has made effective inroads into measuring higher-order thinking skills, another state's testing program may assess relatively low-level skills. Furthermore, because the purpose of this book was to focus on the unintended consequences, the list is not intended to be comprehensive.

We have not explicitly classified many of the consequences as "positive" or "negative" because the interpretation of consequences can vary according to the perspective of the stakeholder. Policy makers who create high-stakes testing policies may find practicing for the tests through increased drill and practice of basic skills to be appropriate and may see it as fulfilling the intended focus of high-stakes reform by focusing teachers and students on the basics. On the other hand, educators often find the drill and practice strategies that are used in test preparation (and other similar teaching practices) to be in opposition to professional standards that call for an increased focus on higher-order thinking skills and problem solving. Thus, the two sets of stakeholders may view the outcomes of high-stakes testing in very different ways. To the policy maker who wants more instruction in the basics, the outcomes are positive. To the educator who is trying to reform the curriculum in accordance with professional standards (such as creating a focus on higher-order thinking), the outcomes are negative. This tension about the goals of education highlights the need for different stakeholders within communities to engage in public debate and discussion.

BROAD STROKES AND FINE LINES

When the entire picture of high-stakes testing is viewed, a number of trends emerge that cross individual cases and enlighten us about how high-stakes testing can impact public education. Clearly, testing focuses teachers on teaching the mechanics of essential skills in reading, writing, and mathematics. For some teachers, this has resulted in improved instruction in these areas. The testing programs have also focused public attention on schools with low-achieving students and, as a result, have made these students more visible and less likely to slip between the cracks and fall further behind. This public attention to low-achieving schools has in some cases brought extra resources and staff development to schools that otherwise may have been ignored. The discourse about low-achieving students has also pulled more parents and community members into the plans for remediation. Ultimately, increased parental involvement can only improve students' learning.

Table 11.1   Consequences of High-Stakes Testing

Consequences for Educational Resources and Reform Efforts

1. Increase in funds spent for testing.
2. Increase in availability of school vouchers.
3. Increase in funds spent for rewards and recognition.
4. Increase in student dropout rates.
5. Increase in student grade level retention.
6. Increase in student referrals for special education programs.
7. Increase in scores in tested subjects.
8. Increase in average cost to educate students.
9. Increase in funds spent for creating, administering, scoring, and interpreting tests.
10. Increase in funds spent for test preparation materials.
11. Increase in funds spent on student remediation for tests.
12. Increase in teacher and administrator time spent preparing and giving tests.
13. Shift in teachers and teacher assistants to classrooms with low-performing students.
14. Shift in focus from professional standards to assessment standards.
15. Increase in the likelihood that socioeconomic class divisions will remain (e.g., low-performing students from poverty stay in poverty).
16. Decrease in social promotion.
17. Differential impact of testing programs on minorities, students with disabilities, students with limited English proficiency, and students from low socioeconomic status communities.
18. Inaccurate interpretations of tests.
19. Increase in summative evaluation and decrease in formative evaluation.
20. Decrease in efforts to promote developmentally appropriate schooling for young children.
21. Increase in focus on schools that underserve students.

Consequences for Students

1. Decrease in graduation rates for students with special needs.
2. Increase in the testing of young children.
3. Decrease in students' confidence.
4. Increase in cheating on tests.
5. Increase in competition between students, classes, and schools.
6. Increase in low-performing students' access to additional help to raise test scores.
7. Increase in students' anxiety.
8. Both increase and decrease in students' motivation.
9. Decrease in students' "love of learning."
10. Increase in test exemptions given to special education students.
11. Increase in labeling of students.
12. Increase in pressure from teachers, principals, and parents for students to raise scores.
13. Increase in use of threats for students to perform well.
14. Increase in number of older students (who were held back) mixed into classes with younger students.
15. Special education students advised to stay home on test days and to avoid taking tested classes.

Table 11.1, continued

Consequences for Teachers

1. Decrease in teacher autonomy.
2. Decrease in teacher creativity.
3. Increase in teachers' levels of stress.
4. Increase in teacher performance for some; decrease in teacher performance for others.
5. Increase in teacher retirement.
6. Increase in teachers' leaving lower-performing schools.
7. Increase in teacher turnover.
8. Increase in professional development focused on assessment programs.
9. Increase in scripted and prescribed teaching.
10. Increase in unethical test preparation by teachers.

Consequences for Instruction

1. Decrease in instruction in nontested subjects such as social studies, art, foreign languages, physical education, science, and health.
2. Increase in external control of instructional approaches and the curriculum.
3. Increase in uniformity in the enacted curriculum.
4. Increase in focus on lower-level skills and knowledge.
5. A narrowed curriculum taught to students.
6. Decrease in number of science laboratories taught.
7. Improvement in the quality of instruction in tested subjects and decline in the quality of instruction in nontested subjects.
8. Increase in externally prescribed instruction.
9. Increase in the time spent taking tests.
10. Increase in standardization of instruction.
11. Increase in use of extrinsic rewards in schools.
12. Increase in use of test motivational activities.
13. Decrease in amount of creative writing by students.
14. Decrease in amount of time spent on instruction.
15. Increase in "drill and practice" teaching approaches.
16. Increase in inquiry-based science teaching in some cases and decrease in inquiry teaching in other cases.
17. Increase in instruction of the mechanics of writing.
18. Increase in amount of science process skills taught when science is tested and decrease in amount of science process skills taught when science is not tested.
19. Increase in skill development instruction.
20. Increase in teaching of test-taking skills.
21. Increase in testing preparation.
22. Increase in amount of time spent teaching higher-level writing.
23. Increase in amount of writing completed by students.
24. A narrowing of teaching focus to testing items.
25. A narrowed range of literature read by students.
26. Shift in focus from learning to a focus on achievement as measured by tests.
27. Teaching time shifted to focus on content areas and items tested.
28. Decrease in developmentally appropriate instructional practices.
29. Decrease in number of guest speakers.

Table 11.1, continued

Consequences for the Community

1. Differential impact on high-poverty schools.
2. Increase in public comparisons of student scores for teachers, schools, and school systems.
3. Increased focus on schools with high numbers of low-performing students.
4. Decrease in average scores on high-stakes tests for minority students as compared to majority students.
5. More conversation with parents about testing.
6. More conversation with parents about what students will be taught.
7. Fewer community service projects.

Unfortunately, many negative consequences of high-stakes tests have also emerged. There is abundant evidence that high-stakes testing programs narrow the curriculum. This narrowing occurs within tested subjects such as mathematics, but it also impacts other subjects such as music, art, and science. Nontested subjects are significantly reduced or eliminated as educators focus on tested subjects.

High-stakes testing programs also result in massive amounts of test preparation. Test preparation initiates an entire chain reaction of other consequences including unethical item teaching, cheating, student anxiety, and loss of instructional time.

For the education community, the shifts in control of what is taught, how it is taught, and who gets high-quality instruction are perhaps the most severe consequences. Whereas states once provided only curriculum frameworks and outlines, they are now dictating the content of instruction down to the most specific detail. This shift in control from local communities to policy makers at the state and national levels has quietly occurred with little debate or recognition. Some testing programs have a provision for state takeover of the school if the students fail to achieve. This means that the state can fire the local principal and all the teachers and hire new personnel. The full implication of this shift in control has yet to be fully realized. Teachers recognize that this shift in control is occurring and are angry over their loss of creativity and flexibility in their teaching.

The consequences of competition among students and schools in academics trigger less obvious types of consequences, including many that have psychological repercussions. Labeling students, teachers, and schools (as "low-performing," "F," etc.) lowers morale, increases stress, and ultimately contributes to increased student dropout rates, higher student retention rates, increased referrals for special education programs, and an educational focus on extrinsic rewards for learning. Schools should entice students to want to learn more and should teach them to love learning, not teach them to fear and avoid learning because they are afraid to fail. Teachers report that the labeling process for schools also results in significant teacher stress and may lead to teachers' leaving the profession.

The focus of testing on cognitive achievement also diminishes the importance of children's emotional and social development. Our experience is that employers seek to hire students and adults who are self-motivated and have social skills. Yet, testing programs do not accommodate or reward students who excel in these areas. Implicitly, students might be learning that these skills are not as important as cognitive achievement.

Finally, reform by high-stakes testing is a very expensive endeavor. The development of a quality test requires significant funds. Funds are also needed for scoring tests; interpreting test results; informing the public of test scores; and educating parents, teachers, and administrators about how to interpret test results. The costs of testing programs may extend further into rewards and recognitions, test preparation materials, testing monitors, and even free breakfasts for students on test days. Given the shortage of dollars for education and the associated lack of adequate classroom space, computers, instructional materials, and teachers, one has to question whether or not the benefits outweigh the financial costs of high-stakes testing programs.

FINAL COMMENTS

Taken as a whole, we believe that the negative consequences of high-stakes testing programs (as currently implemented in most states) outweigh the positive intended consequences. For this reason, we recommend that high-stakes testing programs either be eliminated or considerably altered in form and content. There are means to improve existing testing programs (as we discussed in chapter 10), and these means should be considered seriously and implemented immediately. We cannot allow the political rhetoric of testing to undermine quality public education in this country.

REFERENCE

Linn, R. L. 2000. "Assessments and Accountability." *Educational Researcher* 29, no. 2, 4–14.

Index

Note: An "f" following a page number indicates a figure and a "t" following a page number indicates a table.

About the Authors

M. Gail Jones is associate professor of science education in the School of Education at the University of North Carolina, Chapel Hill, where she conducts research on high-stakes assessment, science education, gender and science, and nanotechnology education. Dr. Jones is a former middle and high school science teacher.

Brett D. Jones is assistant professor of educational psychology in the College of Education at the University of South Florida, St. Petersburg, where he teaches courses in learning and development. His research interests include high-stakes testing and the application of cognitive and motivation theories to teaching and learning.

Tracy Y. Hargrove is assistant professor in the Watson School of Education at the University of North Carolina, Wilmington. Her research interests include authentic assessment, testing and high-stakes accountability, the teaching and learning of elementary and middle school mathematics, and the integration of technology into the mathematics and science curriculum. Dr. Hargrove is a former elementary mathematics teacher and school system technology coordinator.